PUBLISHED IN JUNE 2008

THE TITLE, STYLE OF MAKE-UP
ALMANACK ARE STRI...

Foulsh...
ORIGINAL OLD MOORE'S
Almanack

1697   THE ORIGINAL COPYRIGHT EDITION   **2009**

2009: *A Year for Preparation*

This is a very important year for all of us. Two major periods of volatility are close at hand. The end of a cycle in *2010* may produce a correction similar to the great depression of 1929. And further out I see seismic events in *2012*, which may be as important as the collapse of the Communist Bloc in Eastern Europe. We will have to wait and see whether we are to be at the epicentre of these events.

    It seems to me that it is important here to focus more on *you* in *2009* and less on the nation or world affairs. 2009 may be the last chance to put your finances in order and protect yourself from events that could set us all back.

    Since my *2001* almanack, I have been warning against influences that have encouraged us towards a self-indulgent, credit-driven lifestyle. These are the *identical* influences that produced the 1920's pattern called the Roaring 20s. Of course, history never repeats itself *exactly*. And this is just as well, because it was the Great Depression that followed the Roaring 20s. I have to report that such problems *may* begin in 2009 – Saturn/Uranus is usually a harbinger of financial difficulty. This said, there are also positive signs of restructuring, so even if 2009 is burdensome, it does offer you opportunities.

    Let me re-cap on these influences so that you can decide how you may have been affected personally. Have you been unrealistically optimistic – to the point of being unconcerned? Have you been lax in your social responsibilities – to the point of uncaring? Have you indulged yourself in too much borrowing? Do you tend to focus on yourself to the exclusion of most others? These are attitudes that have become very widespread – right to the top of Government. They have made everybody self-serving, but for Government

© 2008 by OLD MOORE PUBLICATIONS   Tel: (01753) 526769
Printed in England by Apple Web Offset, Warrington, Cheshire
News trade distribution by Seymour 020 7429 4000

A look ahead to events in 2009

Ministers they have produced *wishful thinking/sound-bites* that have failed to produce the successful Government that we have needed.

These are not the kind of attitudes that will help you through 2009 and onwards. You are going to need a more old-fashioned approach to life. If you are more careful in your spending, even save a bit and consciously try to pause for realistic thinking before you act, all will come right for you in the end.

Any changes you make to reorganise your life will be rewarded. There are strong, positive signs for all *new starts* this year. So do make the effort to find advice that helps you sort out any financial problems and put them on a safe, long-term repayment plan. If you don't have any ideas about how to do this, ask for help at your Citizens Advice Bureau. You will find it in the telephone book.

In 2008 we have our businessmen to confront our problems successfully. In 2009, however, there is so much unrealistic thinking around that we cannot count on business yet again. At national level I see a great deal of heated debate about the best way forward between new thinkers and traditionalists. The traditionalists will win, only to be proved quite wrong by 2012. So the confusing influences will continue in their interference.

There are some very positive by-products of these irrational influences that we have to face. They create a perfect climate for imaginative thinkers and creativity. This is very good news for UK Ltd because we have always been particularly creative and inventive. Writing, film-making, computer games creation, fashion design, music, breakthrough technologies and graphic arts will earn us billions in 2009. Our reputation in these areas will grow strongly and all of these activities will become long-term wealth generators for us. Our farmers too will have a particularly good year. They will begin a period of strong profitability whereas, as consumers, we are likely to experience food shortages.

2009 begins with Pluto's final entry into Capricorn. This is a rare combination last seen in 1762 – the start of the Industrial Revolution and the declaration of independence by America. It heralds another dynamic revolutionary period that will require changes of us, yet we will not benefit greatly from them. It is China and in particular India that reap the rewards of this energy. It seems that 2009 will see the first signs of decline for Europe and the West in favour of the new and vigorous new Asian powers. We may also be surprised to see the first signs of positive change in sub-Saharan Africa. Economic potential will begin to be realised. Natural resources will be intelligently exploited and food will become a valuable source of income for its farmers.

We have not been through a challenging period for a good while. 2009 is the time to make a start in positioning yourself for unsettled times ahead. Don't just think about it, *do something* positive to put yourself in a stronger position in 2009.

I wish you well in your planning and success in your plans. Make yourself a good year.

Dr Francis Moore
October 2007

Please name FOULSHAM'S ALMANACK when replying to advertisers

It's Almost Uncanny What This Book Can Do For You!

Test Its Amazing Powers
ABSOLUTELY FREE!

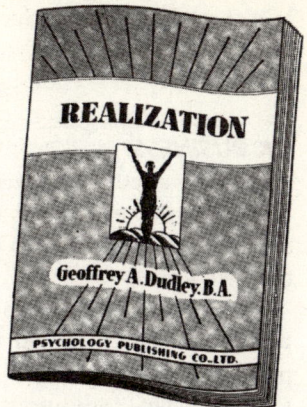

What is the unique influence of this amazing book? From where comes this almost uncanny power to help the timid to a new self-confident personality — the unsuccessful to positions of importance and authority — the sick in their fight back to normal health? It seems incredible! Yet timid, colourless people can simply read this book — and instantly gain courage that performs seeming miracles. Downhearted, frustrated people can scan its pages — and quickly begin to overcome their handicaps. Men and women from every walk of life feel a new vital power surging within them — an irresistible force leading them to undreamed-of success.

SECRET REVEALED

An amazing book! A book that can open exciting, new horizons to everyone who turns its pages. The whole secret lies in this simple fact: everyone has sleeping within himself tremendous unused energy — extraordinary personal powers capable of astonishing development. All you need to do is to release these dormant forces — grasp the full sweep of their amazing powers — then make them ready to do your bidding.

And that is exactly what this unique book can do for you. It shows you how to tap this vast storehouse of the power within. It explains how to release your own vital power — how to magnify it — how to harness it for practical use. The effect is almost immediate. Self-consciousness changes to self-confidence. Timidity gives way to courage. Humility retreats before self-reliance. You gain poise that commands attention.

FREE BOOK

You must see this amazing book for yourself! Test its influence on your own personality. Send for it today — NOW! It's free! No obligation! Just phone 0800 298 7070 free or complete and return the coupon below (no stamp is needed if posted in the U.K.) or send an e-mail (see coupon). Or send your name and address to: The Realization System, (Dept. OMR58T), FREEPOST, Marple, Stockport, SK6 6YA.

WHAT THIS FREE BOOK COULD SHOW YOU
- How to earn more — get a better job!
- How to enjoy vibrant health!
- How to achieve self-confidence!
- How to develop your memory!
- How to relax!
- How to master your emotions!
- How to attain domestic happiness!
- How to realise your ambitions!
- How to win popularity!
- How to build a dynamic personality!

To: The Realization System (Dept OMR58T), FREEPOST, Marple, Stockport SK6 6YA.

Please send me your free Realization Book.

NAME ....
(Mr / Mrs / Miss /Ms)
ADDRESS ....
....
....Postcode...........................
POST TODAY OR CALL 0800 298 7070 FREE
E-mail: OMR58E@bowdenhall.com with your name and postal address
No stamp needed in U.K.

World Affairs

UK BUSINESS
Don't take anything at face value. The leader article points to a year when the world recognises that everybody and every country has been living beyond their means. So you should expect talk of deep recession, coming crashes in the housing market and disasters of other sorts.

You need to look beyond all of this. Remember that for years we in the UK have been having the best of a bad period around the world. 2009 brings nothing to alter our privileged status.

Astrological indications suggest that a great deal of money will be made in farming and related businesses. And that significant investments will enable abandoned mines to be reopened and other dormant opportunities to produce energy. Global oil prices are likely to be as fickle as the financial markets themselves. And to some, oil will be as valuable as gold. 2009 may well prove that the oil-producing states that have encouraged these highest ever prices will experience repercussions. It may be that by the end of the year we will see the lowest prices for a long time.

THE UNITED KINGDOM
2009 is not scheduled to be an election year in the UK. We should have to wait until 2010–11. It follows that politics will be very much a matter of shadow boxing, with party leaders rehearsing the moves they will make come the election. Bearing this in mind, the policies that are important to our economic climate are likely to be 'steady-as-she-goes'. We may need more than this.

We can certainly expect clashes between ecological groups and those who want the UK economy at the top of our list. Harsh realities will be faced and new values will begin to emerge. We will find our way forward in 2009 with new sense of nationalism that England, in particular, has not experienced for a very long time. And a greater sense of community will begin to emerge, though we will need to manage this carefully.

THE USA
As I write in October 2007, the beginning of 2009 in the USA looks very distant. The candidates have not been chosen for the Presidential campaign and everything looks too close to make predictions now. The horoscope for the inauguration at noon on 20 January helps a bit. To begin with, there are excellent indications for peace and prosperity. From this I can predict that the incoming President will benefit from of a huge wave of

optimistic, 'feel-good' factor – from around the world. And I expect a flurry of welcome policy announcements that create the illusion of change. But as we already know, 2009 is not going to be a year of change. It is going to be a year of preparation. It is more likely that the US will believe that it is setting off on a new course but will hit the economic buffers. In 2009 the US faces a 'reality check' that makes itself felt in many ways. The new President will need great wisdom and the ability to act on the evidence, not the unrealistic visions and dreams that have been our leaning for so many years.

I also see a pronounced backlash connected to global warming issues. And there is little doubt of a tinderbox situation that produces deteriorating relations between the United States and Russia.

RUSSIA

News forecaster predictions of a new 'cold war' are little short of incredible. And any threats identified by Western journalists to Russian democracy will also prove greatly exaggerated. So what do I see for Russia?

During 2009 there will be some instability and uncertainty. Russia will fare no better than the rest of us. And there may be some provocation from the new US administration that is trying to assert itself. But far more important to Russia than any of this petty nonsense is the entry of Pluto into Capricorn. This repeats a similar pattern that we saw when the Soviet Union collapsed. And it links to the Russian horoscope that reveals its pride and nationalism. The resurgence of Russian power and influence in the last few years has been a preview of what is to begin in 2009. For a long time, the US has been able to behave as if it was the only superpower. But this is about to change. We will now see Russia retake its position on the world stage in 2009. Western policy makers will need to understand this and change their attitudes.

PALESTINE AND THE MIDDLE EAST

This region of the world has been at war for 3,000 years. However, there are slight indications of the beginnings of change. Israel may no longer be able to rely so heavily on US backing, as it has done in recent years. And I expect new pressures from unexpected directions to force her towards the negotiating table. What problems do arise are more likely to come from the Palestinians. Alas, it looks unlikely that peace in this unstable region is about to emerge – though some optimistic signs are to be found for sure.

Iraq may find some kind of more uneasy stability – though its burgeoning democracy seems likely to be the first casualty. There seems to be no real end to the problems in Afghanistan, which are likely to rumble on for years yet. And Iran? I predict more of the same. Iran will continue to be a country that is insular, brooding and potentially dangerous to her neighbours.

2009 – The Year of the Ox

Chinese astrology works on a slightly different clock to that used in the more familiar Western branch of the study. As a result the commencement of the Chinese New Year differs from year to year and, in 2009, does not begin until 29 January. For most of January, therefore, the world is still under the rulership of the gregarious, volatile Rat, and so political intrigues, changes and reforms are to be expected.

The onset of the Year of the Ox, however, should bring a slight calming of those events that had previously proved to be unpredictable. A greater sense of stability is likely in some quarters, and where changes do take place on the world scene, they are likely to have been anticipated and therefore to inspire a greater sense of confidence. This is because the Ox is associated with the steady and hard-working sign of Capricorn. In both the Western and Chinese systems the sign is said to imply determination and a slow but certain path towards the ultimate achievement of goals.

In Chinese astrology, one of the four elements – Earth, Air, Fire and Water – is also allocated in rotation to each year. The element associated with the Ox during 2009 is Earth, and this does ensure that a degree of thoughtful, contemplative and practical action attaches itself to the normally quiet periods that the Ox governs. The combination of the Ox and Earth could conspire to make 2009 a fairly positive period but one that is likely to be based on consideration and sensible actions.

On the world stage as a whole, it is possible that a few long-term problems will be talked about more seriously, though the chance of immediate solutions is somewhat limited under the rule of the Ox. Widespread social reforms are unlikely and years ruled by the Ox can sometimes bring periods of famine to developing countries. Since the Ox also brings application, such problems, when they do arise, are often dealt with sensibly by the more developed world and we can, therefore, look towards a year of greater responsibility generally.

If you were born under the sign of the Ox, which generally speaking would mean your birthday fell in 1925, 1937, 1949, 1961, 1973, 1985, 1997 or 2009, you can expect an extra boost in the year ahead and a little more than usual in the way of success. As an industrious Ox, you always do your best and though you might not think or act as quickly as some of the people around you, you do get where you want to be in the end. In love, you are constant and reliable, and would do almost anything for someone who is truly important to you.

When it comes to the practical side of life you are second-to-none and people will always call on you when things need to be done. You are very capable, adaptable and always willing to get your hands dirty if necessary. In the year ahead your varied talents are likely to be used in a variety of different ways and it is highly likely, no matter what your age, that you will be studying and doing all you can to gain new skills that will be extremely useful to you in the longer-term future.

Please name FOULSHAM'S ALMANACK when replying to advertisers

YOUR VERY OWN PERSONAL
CHINESE HOROSCOPE
Secret Insights & Predictions from the Mystic Far East

Over the centuries millions of people have been deeply affected by the **oldest horoscope in the world**, and even today people are still benefiting from the knowledge they gain from the **unique traditional Chinese** horoscope – and its revelations on Happiness, Love, Success and Health.

Based on your date of birth this **Original Chinese Horoscope** from **Old Moore's venerable friend** Kuang C. Wang gives you a unique insight into yourself and your future – a truly fascinating and in-depth **personal character analysis plus predictions and forecasts** of which you should be aware.

Your personal **Original Chinese Horoscope** is accurately drawn up for you alone. It reveals at great length your abilities and talents, your limits and weaknesses. Even your future trends and influences are all accurately and confidentially worked out for you from your personal data.

All this at an unbelievable low price – 6 months at only £15.90 or 12 months at only £25.90 post free.

JUST SOME OF OUR TESTIMONIALS:

"The Chinese signs are more understandable and more logical compared with the common approach." Prof. E.K.

"The accurate horoscope you made for me completely hit the truth." M.S.

"It is phenomenal how your analysis has come true." S.G.

Don't miss this unique chance to learn about everything that the future holds in store for you, including your lucky days and numbers. Don't delay, order today and bring to light the understanding of your past, present & future. *Kuang C. Wang*
(Please allow 28 days for delivery.)

To: Kuang C. Wang, P.O. Box 71, Bedford, MK40 2WR   840001

YES! Please draw up my **Original Chinese Horoscope**

Mrs ☐   Miss ☐   Ms ☐   Mr ☐

☐ for 6 months at £15.90 post free (Overseas £20 or $30 USA)
☐ for 12 months at £25.90 post free (Overseas £30 or $45 USA)

Name: _____

Address: _____
_____

Please print your birth details

Date and year: _____

Time (if known): _____

I enclose crossed cheque/PO for £ _____   Place: _____

If you prefer not to receive mailings from companies other than those connected to K. C. Wang, tick the box ☐

Dragon 龍
Snake 蛇
Horse 馬
Goat 羊
Rabbit 兔
Buffalo 牛
Tiger 虎
Pig 猪
Monkey 猴
Rooster 鷄
Dog 犬
Rat 鼠

Oscar-winning leading lady

Cate Blanchett

PA Photos

Despite a glittering showbiz career, this star of exotic filmic creations such as *Elizabeth, The Lord of the Rings* and *The Aviator* is very much rooted in reality. She was born Catherine Álise Blanchett, in Melbourne, Australia on 14 May 1969, giving her Sun in Taurus, Mercury in Gemini and Venus in Aries. A set of contradictions, she once described herself as being both extrovert and a wallflower, which chimes well with a combination of earth and fire signs. Taurus, the earthy, realist achiever, is here to build and wants things to last (Cate has a deep-felt concern for environmental issues), while Saturn makes her patient, purposeful and able to get results.

Her most powerful astrological configuration (the Sun–Neptune opposition) is one that is found on many an actor's chart. Neptune rules the imaginative realm, and what better way for the Sun to express itself than through this creative and potentially lucrative medium? The combination with the sheer determination of Sun/Saturn Taurus and a strong element of self-belief (the Sun in auspicious contact to Jupiter–Pluto) indicates success. This Sun–Jupiter–Pluto link facilitates useful career contacts and provides the power to influence others – no surprise then that Cate has been cited as one of *Time* magazine's '100 Most Influential People'!

Cate's more gregarious side stems from Venus in Aries (tending towards impulsiveness in love), indicating a no-nonsense woman of action. Honest, instantly friendly, loyal and with firm principles, with Mars in Sagittarius she also has a love of travel and a spirit of adventure. With Mercury (the mind) in curious Gemini, she needs a partner with whom she can discuss ideas and philosophies, and Mercury making an opposing angle to fiery Mars, inflames her views with energy and certainty. She is determined to stand up for what is right, and Mars in harsh contact to intense Pluto makes her unafraid of a fight!

Such strengths may be needed in 2009 as the presence of both Pluto (drastic action) and Uranus (restlessness) signifies radical change. Flashpoints are likely in January and July as Pluto contacts Saturn, calling for big alterations to her personal life. Opposition transits by Uranus in March and June require her to use her judgement, neither rushing into new opportunities, nor letting opportunities slip by. August sees restrictions on freedom and a need to focus energies. Early September may see Cate impatient with the way things are, wanting to make a big statement, possibly related to eco-matters. Late September and November see two strong Saturn conjunctions, which could indicate struggles with authority or offers of acting parts related to prison, poverty or politics. This year brings the need for life-changes and Cate will have to fight her Taurean liking for stability.

Old Moore can help you

0906 11 94 021
Old Moore Speaks To You Live

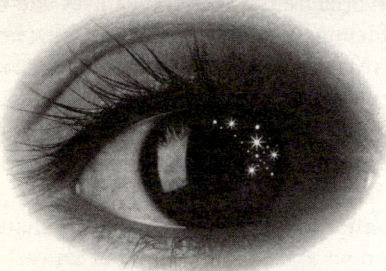

I am Dr Francis Moore, the world's most successful seer, and I have some wonderful people working with me. They discuss things with me when I am in difficulty.

My intuition can't work at 100% every day and I just need to talk things through sometimes before the correct prediction jumps out at me.

Perhaps my people can help you too. My team members will talk to you about your questions if you phone them on my psychic line. Or they may even see something for you by way of a personal prediction or two.

I've been widowed for five years and I rang your psychic line as I wondered if anyone new would come into my life as I have been very lonely. The psychic told me I would not have to go looking for a relationship as it would come and find me in an unusual way. She said his hobby was with bikes and travel and he would need my help. A month later I was in my kitchen when I heard this almighty crash. A man on a motorbike had been hit from behind and crashed into my garden. I ended up going with him to the hospital. After several weeks in hospital and many visits we have become close friends and companions; my life is no longer empty. – Theresa from Mablethorpe

After many years of working in a large company I wanted to take early retirement and an opportunity arose to try something different. The lease had come up on a village pub, where I had plenty of experience as a customer but little behind the bar. My wife and I were apprehensive but my instinct was urging me to take a risk. Your psychic quickly put me at ease and got straight to the heart of the matter. She saw a bright, prosperous business that would give me lots of pleasure and where I would get support and encouragement. It was the best move we could have made. We've a team of happy staff and the gratitude of a bustling village community. – Alan from West Horndon

Love? Health? Career? Money?
Relationships? Life?

Calls cost £1.50 per minute. You must be over 18 to use this service. Consultants are available 24 hours a day, 7 days a week. All calls are recorded. Helpline: 0113 384 7008.

Daniel Craig

PA Photos

More than one critic has suggested that the most recent James Bond to hit the silver screen is more like the true character of the Ian Fleming novels than any of his previous incarnations. But is that because Daniel Craig is a talented actor, because those cold blue eyes add to the impression of Fleming's enigmatic and complex hero or are there other reasons to be found in his birth chart?

Daniel Craig was born in Chester, England on 2 March 1968, which puts him firmly under the Sun sign of Pisces. One wouldn't normally think of a Piscean as a ruthless spy who is licensed to kill, but this is not the only important astrological association in this chart.

Having shown an aptitude for acting at an early age, Craig joined the National Youth Theatre at 16, and roles in *Lara Croft: Tomb Raider* and *Road to Perdition* followed. He is a man with a mission, thanks to a Mars–Saturn conjunction in Aries, which also demonstrates a physicality ideally suited to 007. Aries is where Mars loves to be most, which makes Daniel a natural leader and may account for a tendency to be short tempered. He wants things to be a certain way and expects others to work as tirelessly as he does to get things right.

Venus in Aquarius may help to explain some of the relationship problems that Craig has experienced. He has exacting standards and a slightly chauvinistic side, and though he can be a people person, he is enigmatic too. Pisces is a natural chameleon and can change its colour to suit the prevailing circumstances. He clearly admires beauty in his partners but what he really needs is someone perceptive enough to understand him fully.

One is left with the impression of a strong jawed, maybe not classically handsome but immensely magnetic person, of the sort that would be an asset in a crisis. The planets in his chart, and especially Mars and Saturn, indicate a deep masculinity, but are balanced by their trine to Venus, giving integrity allied to strength.

Both Daniel Craig's chart and the box office ratings indicate continued success on the big screen but his need for public approbation may mean more appearances on the stage as he eventually find films leave him too distant from his audience.

While even the most experienced astrologer may struggle to understand the person behind this chart, there are certainly indications of hidden depths and a yearning desire to do something extraordinary, both for himself and for the world. Might we find Daniel Craig eventually associated with politics, world news and genuine situations of conflict? Though James Bond is just a part he plays, if 007 ever did have a birth chart of his own it might not look too different to this one.

Please name FOULSHAM'S ALMANACK when replying to advertisers

The Power of Speaking Things into Existence
It was the basis of Egyptian magick.

WHAT ONE SEEKS CAN BE SPOKEN INTO EXISTENCE!
To the Egyptians, this wasn't mumbo jumbo, but *metaphysical science*.
YOU CAN 'SPEAK THINGS INTO EXISTENCE'.
You are limited only by the boundaries of your thought!
You can change your circumstances.
You don't need anyone else to do it for you.
This publication shows **how it is done**.
You can do it!
A child can do it!
This publication unravels the mystery and SPEAKS THE TRUTH.
And *the truth is simple!*
Example 1: **Christina J., 34, from Jersey, wanted a way out of debt and misery. SHE SPOKE HER WAY OUT OF IT and turned her life around in two months!**
This publication **explains** exactly how to get out of the **present mess** with this Egyptian method.
And if you are already doing well, shows **how you can make it even better!**
Example 2: **Jeff S., 39, from Dover was in turmoil when his wife walked out. Fifteen years of marriage down the drain.**
His wife walked back in when he learnt the Power of Speaking Things into Existence.
No magick words are supplied, what you speak is in your own tongue: but you will be shown the ASTONISHING POWER OF SPEECH.
When you speak in a certain way – invoking – your desire – the Universe listens!
The Egyptians believed it!
Example 3: **Katy, 57, from Cambridge, found bankruptcy staring her in the face with the closure of her shop. Skyrocketing costs made it impossible for her to carry on.**
She didn't go under – instead she *spoke her way into prosperity*! Six months later she owned two shops in the same town and is planning to open a third!
Why should success elude you? Why should you always have to scrimp and save?
Why do you not ever win anything?
YOU CAN REVERSE THE STATUS QUO!
You can become the successful and envied one!
Example 4: **Peter B., 49, from Chester, longed for a certain lady who seemed completely unobtainable.**
Within a short time, she became his lover!
This publication shows you how *to focus the universe on your needs*.
Words are powerful things!
They can manifest your desires!
YOU CAN SPEAK YOUR WAY TO PROSPERITY ... LOVE ... HAPPINESS ... and whatever else you have set your heart on!
There was a time when one could be imprisoned for publishing and reading what is here. BECAUSE THOSE IN AUTHORITY COULD NEVER TOLERATE DEFENCE-LESS INDIVIDUALS POSSESSING SUCH POTENT KNOWLEDGE!
This knowledge can *set you free*.

Free of limitation ... free of heartbreak ... free of suffering.
'Abracadabra!' goes the pantomime magician and by magic a wish materialises!
Behind every lie, lies a TRUTH!
The Egyptian magician understood the awesome power of words. YOU CAN NOW EXPLOIT THIS HIDDEN POWER!
No harm can befall you.
Example 5: **Betty T., 72, of Bristol, dreamt of going on a 6-week luxury cruise, but had no means of making it true. She tried the Egyptian metaphysical secret and was astonished!**
She not only got her cruise, *but booked a second one*!
We think, 'Well, others might be able to do it, but I can't. I'm just unlucky'.
THAT IS A LIE!
NEVER LIE TO YOURSELF!
OPEN YOURSELF TO *THE TRUTH*.
Nothing in this life is quite what it seems, until you realise what formidable power could be in your grasp.
You can become *an initiate of the Cosmos*.
You can now be initiated into your *own limitless potential* through the truth expounded in this remarkable booklet.
We repeat: IT IS EASY.
Example 6: **Freddie H., 24, from Camden, was bitterly disappointed at being turned down for a project he desperately wanted to be involved in.** He sunk into depression.
Discovering this power, he felt a burden lifted from his shoulders, and 'miraculously' he was later admitted to the project even though he was previously told there was 'no chance'!
YOU DO NOT HAVE TO TAKE 'NO' FOR AN ANSWER!
Doors are forced open when you tap into hidden metaphysical realms.
It seems crazy, 'Speaking Things into Existence'.
How can it be?
Well, it is. And it *happens all the time*. But we don't see it, for we are conditioned by what others *want us to believe*!
You need to know exactly how much money you want.
You have to be absolutely specific about the person who interests you and the part you want them to play in your life.
You need to be specific as to how you want your health improved.
What you desire is within your grasp and is far CLOSER to realisation than you think!
It *isn't madness*! You can SPEAK THINGS INTO EXISTENCE!
Failure only becomes fact when we *cease to believe*.
Are you *serious* about success? Do you seriously want prosperity, happiness, love, better health, and all the other things that make life worthwhile?
YOU CAN SPEAK THESE THINGS INTO EXISTENCE.
Give yourself a break.
If a child can do it, you can.
To receive this information please simply quote 'SPEAKING THINGS INTO EXISTENCE' and send **£9.99**.

Please send **£9.99** cheque or postal order made payable to 'Finbarr' – to: **Finbarr (OE), Folkestone, Kent CT20 2QQ.**
Overseas send £15. Catalogue of unusual books 50p. PLEASE GIVE YOUR NAME AND ADDRESS.

Please name FOULSHAM'S ALMANACK when replying to advertisers

MICHAEL FRANCOIS

Considered one of the world's leading psychics
I HAVE THE POWER TO HELP YOU SOLVE YOUR PROBLEMS
Tel: 0207 387 4314

I can help with problems involving:
LOVE • EXAMS • MONEY • CURSES
MARRIAGE • CAREER SUCCESS
PROTECTION
UNWANTED INFLUENCES CLEARED

I have in my office documented evidence of my readings for various celebrities; Heads of State, Nobles, Actors, Actresses, TV Presenters, Sports Stars, etc., etc. (Evidence of all these has been submitted to the British Advertising Standards Authority.) The list is almost endless.

Dozens of testimonials arriving every week.

You are amazing!
"Everything I asked for has happened, thank you so much ... What I feel for you is very special, you are amazing." (Mrs. R.O., Florida U.S.A.)
"The accuracy of your reading has left me dumbfounded – absolutely spot on." (Mr. S.R., Scotland)
"My lover and I are now reunited, do say thank you to all of your team." (Miss T.E., Manchester)

By addressing yourself to me you will not be disappointed, because I will personally reply, sending you a personal reading carried out specifically with helping you in mind.

My work (the reputation of which surpasses all boundaries, and my references are without doubt my best guarantees) will bring you at last the help that you have the right to expect from a professional occultist and clairvoyant. My role is to **help you** resolve **your** problems by improving **your** life. All my energy is put to use to solve **your** problems because I sincerely want to and am able to help.

Please name FOULSHAM'S ALMANACK when replying to advertisers

The purchase of this excellent specialist publication is proof of your sensitivity to using esoteric forces to help guide you through life. Although this interest undoubtedly gives you an advantage over the vast majority of the general public, there are times when this interest alone is not enough. Knowing the basics of these sciences is one thing, but being able to take advantage of the benefits they may bring in a tangible way is another. For this, only a top specialist can guarantee success.

My reputation is such that I cannot afford to let you down. In my reading, all aspects of your life will be covered, your character and personality (hidden strengths and weaknesses), auspicious or unfavourable phases, professional development, the area involving your affections – union, marriage, separation – and of course, advice on how to achieve ultimate success in any domain in life. My advice is sacred and you have already begun acquiring it, now it is up to you to contact me. I look forward to hearing from you and leading you towards a brighter future and wish you all the best until then.

Michael Francois

AVAILABLE IMMEDIATELY
Personal readings by appointment – Call Now 0207 387 4314

Michael Francois, 118 Piccadilly, Mayfair, London W1J 7NW

Priority Postal Readings by sending off the coupon below.

My name ....

My address ....

My date, my place and if possible my hour of birth ....

My most desired wish ....

I enclose payment of £20 by way of cheque/postal order/registered cash, payable to Michael Francois.

www.michaelfrancois.com

Your 2009 Birthday Guide

By working with the major astrological influences, you can take control and give your life a better focus. These personal guides show you how to make the most of the positive times and also indicate which days need to be handled with care.

ARIES BORN PEOPLE
Birthdays: 21 March to 20 April inclusive
Planet: Mars. Birthstone: Diamond. Lucky day: Tuesday

Keynote for the Year: *Look out for new opportunities to explore socially, and treat any increase in duties and responsibilities as character building.*

JANUARY: Main Trends: 3–4 Look to casual conversations for personal fulfilment and keep your ears open for useful information. **19–21** Friendships and social relationships are favourably highlighted, so be sure to get the most from group encounters. **22–23** Focus on moving forwards with professional and business developments as the way ahead should be clearly indicated. **Key Dates: Highs 3–5; 31** Making genuine progress and getting proper results may become easier. Why not make some bold decisions? **Lows 16–17** Keep important plans on ice – this may not be the best time to force your way ahead.

FEBRUARY: Main Trends: 3–5 Your love and social life may be rewarding – get out there and enjoy yourself. **6–7** Take care to be more compromising than usual as contact with friends and associates could unearth minor tensions. **19–20** Your potential for material success may have dwindled. Concentrate on reviewing the past and quietly planning out the future. **Key Dates: Highs 1; 27–28** Good luck should be yours for the taking – but you'll never know until you take the initiative. **Lows 12–14** Beware of impractical ideas and hasty decisions affecting work routines.

MARCH: Main Trends: 10–11 Private matters may be rewarding. Make the most of your analytical ability to work out what is on a partner's mind. **15–16** Use this energy to gather vital information. Don't let the past hold you back or prevent you from projecting a confident image. **20–21** Capitalise on your strong self-esteem by making new beginnings and taking the lead, whether in business or romance. **Key Dates: Highs 26–27** Put your best foot forward during this lucky phase. **Lows 8–9** Your spirits may be low – take it easy.

APRIL: Main Trends: 12–13 Friendship is highlighted. Look to group co-operation to advance your career. **19–20** Emphasise the material world – focus on money in order to make financial progress. **25–26** With rash Mars in your sign you'll probably take a bolder approach to life – be prepared for some admiring your courage and honesty, while others may see you as outspoken and reckless! **Key Dates: Highs 23–24** Take advantage of this phase of luck and considerable personal influence to talk influential people around to your way of thinking. **Lows 8–9** Don't expect everything to go smoothly and be prepared for delays.

MAY: Main Trends 13–14 Look out for chances for financial improvement and concentrate on major decisions as these should bring excellent results. **20–21** While communication issues are positively highlighted and you may find yourself in agreeable company, take the chance to negotiate successfully. **30–31** Make the most of savings or investments to bring financial rewards, but do resist hasty decisions. **Key Dates: Highs 20–21** Take advantage of your good luck to get what you want. **Lows 5–7** There may be obstacles in your way, so be prepared to abandon plans and start again.

Please name FOULSHAM'S ALMANACK when replying to advertisers

Sugar Spells

Carole Colmore writes –

It was my great grandmother who taught me the old country magick of Sugar Spells. A wise lady, she lived a happy and contented life, and would always say 'A little sprinkling of sugar can sweeten your luck'.

She was right. I have been blessed over and over again by this simple piece of folklore.

I use sugar all the time to sweeten my life (though I don't take it with my tea!).

Twice in the last six months alone I have won £17,000 on horses (that's about $33,000 in American money). I enter various lotteries and whilst I am yet to get 'the big one' I am not complaining. I get back, on average, £9 on every £1 bet.

Three months ago I unexpectedly found myself out of a job when my employers went bankrupt. But I don't know if I really do want to find another job, for there is just so much to enjoy in life – and sugar spells just keep sweetening it.

My brother was desperate to get a particular job. I gave him a sugar spell to do. He laughed saying, 'This is nonsense!' I said try it anyway – what's there to lose?

He got the job – and learnt that there were 33 other applicants for it.

I do competitions all the time. I have three TV sets and two DVD players; all won as prizes. I got my washing machine the same way.

Two years ago I won a luxury two-week Mediterranean cruise as a first prize.

I could go on, but really, you need to try these sugar spells for yourself.

Each spell is simplicity itself. All you need to have to hand is a teaspoonful of sugar. This is not black magick; and anyone of any faith or creed can do it without compromising their beliefs. They are safe and easy – a child could do them. There are no 'magick words' to recite, and no candles or equipment of any kind. No visualising either!

I don't believe in coincidence. I see people everywhere with bad luck, their lives dogged by trouble. It is hard to believe they have a guardian angel looking over them. On the other hand, some folk just seem to have everything go their way.

I am not suggesting that they are performing spells – and would they tell you if they were? – but I know my luck isn't coincidence.

Money is not everything of course. When my best friend was beset by a stomach ulcer I urged her to try a sugar spell. The ulcer disappeared completely after three weeks.

I have always been prone to asthma; a couple of years ago it seemed particularly bad. The sweetening spell brought me relief.

Obviously you shouldn't use these spells as a substitute for medication; but I do ask you to have an open mind. I don't believe in coincidence.

I cast a sugar spell on behalf of my ailing aunt. She made a complete recovery.

Her cat suffered a mysterious stomach disorder which baffled the vet. I loved this cat and thought there was nothing to lose by performing a sugar spell. Two weeks later the cat was back to her bright self: eating well, her insides working perfectly.

Perhaps it was 'coincidence', but I don't believe in coincidence.

Each sugar spell in my booklet takes no more than a few minutes to do. You may think it's nonsense – but what if it isn't?

A friend of mine thought it was silly. But she was crazy about a fellow who showed little interest in her. 'OK – even if it's "silly" like you say, why not try it for a laugh and see what happens?' A week later he asked her out. They subsequently became lovers.

My own boyfriend was paying too much interest in a friend for my comfort. I did my little sugar spell, and even I was astonished at his sudden indifference to her.

My great grandmother told me how her brother was devastated by his wife's departure with another man. A sugar spell was cast. She left the other man and returned to her husband.

Another time my own brother was bothered by a neighbour who kept intruding. **The neighbour stopped bothering him almost immediately the sugar spell was in place.**

If you are in dispute with a neighbour a sugar spell can give you the advantage. It can also make someone move away.

Sugar Spells can be applied to a host of situations: Obtaining a payrise ... bringing peace and harmony into the home ... protection from burglary ... making someone pay back what they owe; or return to you what is rightfully yours. This magick can also be used to end a relationship, or to get someone out of your life. On the other hand sugar spells can be used to heal a relationship.

They were a man and wife but their marriage was heading for disaster ... in one last attempt to save it she cast a sugar spell. Not only did the 'impossible' occur, but they became happier than they had been at any time!

It's time to 'sweeten *your* life'!

Please send **£5.99** cheque or postal order made payable to 'Finbarr' – to: **Finbarr (OSS), Folkestone, Kent CT20 2QQ.**
Overseas send £9. If you are in a real hurry add 65p and write 'PRIORITY' on face of envelope.
PLEASE INCLUDE YOUR NAME AND ADDRESS.

Aries: a guide to your good-luck days

JUNE: Main Trends: 6–7 Capitalise on money matters and assistance from others to attract the good things in life. 14–15 You should be able to deal with several different tasks with some success, so try out new schemes, especially in the work place. 21–22 Concentrate on the home environment and your domestic surroundings and look to the past for the most beneficial results. **Key Dates: Highs** 16–18 Capitalise on your luck by taking risks. **Lows** 2–3 Don't expect material achievement, but try to be satisfied with what you've got.

JULY: Main Trends: 3–4 Look for rewards in matters that are close to the heart, especially at home. Make this a special time for yourself and your nearest and dearest. 5–6 Take advantage of this communication peak to put forward any major proposals you are considering – but avoid distractions! 22–23 An auspicious time for creative pursuits, so show the world what you can do. Focus on romantic issues too. **Key Dates: Highs** 14–15 A personal boost when you should push ahead with important matters while you are on a roll. **Lows** 26–27 Beware of unfocused thinking or getting too carried away with an idea.

AUGUST: Main Trends: 1–2 Avoid any reckless decision-making – if you aren't thoroughly organised a major plan could miss the target. 7–8 Focus on the home, whether entertaining guests or considering improvements. 21–22 Take the opportunity to consolidate career developments and capitalise on your organising skills. **Key Dates: Highs** 10–11 Make the most of this lucky time to get the very best from life. **Lows** 23–24 Real advancement may be thin on the ground, so don't get involved in anything risky. Lay low and rest.

SEPTEMBER: Main Trends: 17–18 Practical affairs should be more stable. Be sure to benefit from the input of colleagues. 21–22 Use your abilities as a go-between or mediator, and work too with those in authority who can help you to move on. 23–24 Your social life and partnerships are highlighted. Take advantage of your abilities as a shrewd negotiator in business. **Key Dates: Highs** 6–7 Take a step into the unknown as this phase may assist you in getting to your chosen destination. **Lows** 19–20 Be cautious about important decisions during this unlucky time.

OCTOBER: Main Trends: 14–15 Enjoy joint projects or one-to-one encounters, particularly in your love life, where you should find you are very popular! 22–24 Concentrate your energies on re-organising and renewing your present circumstances – focus only on essentials and make way for the new. 28–29 Be adaptable and accept that something may have passed its sell-by date and no longer be of much use. **Key Dates: Highs** 3–4; 31 Capitalise on your ideas and put your luck to the test. **Lows** 16–18 You may have difficulty getting ahead or connecting with others, so consider spending some time alone.

NOVEMBER: Main Trends: 8–9 Look to close relationships for a change for the better, and to partners for financial help. 16–17 Give way to a strong urge for freedom – all matters cultural and intellectual can bring out the best in you. 22–23 A favourable time for travelling and widening personal horizons, perhaps through the interesting people you meet. **Key Dates: Highs** 1; 27–28 Make the best of progressive and promising matters either socially or in business. **Lows** 13–14 Suspend major decisions while you lack energy or enthusiasm.

DECEMBER: Main Trends: 1–2 Travel and mental interests may well be rewarding, so consider a complete change of scenery. 5–6 Look to brand new information to help you on the way towards personal objectives. 20–21 Make the most of your good, practical ideas for professional improvement and move towards steady progress in your career. **Key Dates: Highs** 24–26 Capitalise on your considerable abilities to get what you want. **Lows** 10–11 You could be feeling rather lacklustre and should avoid too many commitments. Rest if at all possible.

Please name FOULSHAM'S ALMANACK when replying to advertisers

Your very own personal horoscope by Old Moore

The timeless wisdom of **Old Moore** *can now be interpreted by computer – to give you an astounding wealth of insights and revelations.*

At last, the huge analytical power of the computer has been harnessed to the legendary forecasting skills of **Old Moore**.

By revealing the mysteries held within your own astrological chart, you will gain a unique insight into yourself and find a new path to your future which you yourself can influence.

It is based on the **Old Moore** prediction system, which has proved to be uniquely successful and accurate for over three hundred years.

Now it focuses entirely on *YOU*. The result is your very own *character profile and forecast horoscope* for the next twelve months.

Send off the coupon below with your remittance of £17.00, and enjoy a unique view of your future.

12-month Horoscope Book – personal to you – for only £17.00 INCLUDING P&P.

✳ **Most detailed astral reading of its kind.**

✳ **CHARACTER PROFILE explores the depths of your true self.**

✳ **PERSONAL FORECAST predicts ways to improve your happiness and success.**

✳ **In a tradition of accurate forecasting since 1697.**

YOUR DATE WITH DESTINY...

UNIQUE GIFT IDEA – SEND THIS COUPON NOW!

To BJA, PO Box 1321, SLOUGH PDO, Berkshire SL1 5YD. I enclose £17.00 for my **Old Moore** Personal Horoscope (Overseas £19.00, €30 or $37.95 USA.)
Make cheques payable to BJA.   (Please allow 28 days for delivery.)

NAME _____

ADDRESS _____

_____

_____

POST CODE _____

Please print your birth details:

DATE AND YEAR _____

TIME (IF KNOWN) _____

PLACE _____

If you prefer not to receive mailings from companies other than those connected to Old Moore, please tick the box ❏

Taurus: your day-to-day guide to 2009

TAURUS BORN PEOPLE
Birthdays: 21 April to 21 May inclusive
Planet: Venus. Birthstone: Emerald. Lucky day: Friday

Keynote for the Year: *Make the most of a real chance to further your career growth over the next 12 months, and be prepared to make a far more serious commitment to your love life.*

JANUARY: Main Trends: 3–4 Focus on new and promising social developments to get the most from friendships – the bigger the occasion, the better. 21–22 Capitalise on your career and push for what you want. Look to the outside world to supply your needs! 23–24 Communication matters may reach a peak, so take full advantage of this favourable time for personal discussions. Try to have a more inclusive, open-minded attitude in order to be successful. **Key Dates: Highs** 6–7 Be sure to capitalise on this lucky phase. **Lows** 18–20 You may lack enthusiasm, so try to avoid major obligations.

FEBRUARY: Main Trends: 2–3 This may not be a time of fulfilment. You may require tact and patience to preserve the status quo in personal encounters. 4–5 As the number of professional events increases, be cautious and don't take anything for granted or overlook important details. 19–20 Concentrate on group involvements and you may well get a cordial reception from others. **Key Dates: Highs** 2–3 Don't be afraid to gamble with your time and energy, as you should be able to accomplish lots with minor effort on your part. **Lows** 15–16 Don't struggle to accomplish your aims – kick back and review things, rather than take on too much.

MARCH: Main Trends: 8–9 Look to your social life for reasons to smile and be ready for new and inspirational encounters. 12–13 Concentrate on independent tasks where you can make your own decisions as you may struggle to agree with others at this time. 20–21 This is the time for self-sacrifice and putting yourself at others' disposal rather than trying to maintain a high social profile. **Key Dates: Highs** 1–2; 28–30 Follow your heart and let intuition guide you on the path to progress. **Lows** 14–15 You may struggle to get your own way, so slow things down and keep it simple.

APRIL: Main Trends: 12–13 Maximise your potential in the professional sphere. Your ability to enlist the help of others may affect your career opportunities. 19–20 Be sure to benefit from your increased self-confidence and this period of dynamic action. 22–23 Be prepared for a downside to certain plans and ambitions, and a lack of vitality. Avoid impatience and any minor accidents that are caused by this. **Key Dates: Highs** 25–26 Maximise your potential at this time and be aware that a word in the right ear might speed progress. **Lows** 10–12 Try to wind down when it comes to major objectives and recharge your batteries.

MAY: Main Trends: 13–15 Put your ingenuity and versatility to good use by attending to a multitude of interests. 20–21 Be sure to benefit from financial opportunities. Use this lucky time to build on new beginnings. 30–31 An energetic phase, during which you may tend to be competitive with associates. If a battle of wills should occur, be sure the issue is worth fighting over. **Key Dates: Highs** 22–23 There is much to be done, so get an early start with significant matters, whether personal or professional. **Lows** 8–9 Keeping body and soul together may prove difficult. Don't be too hard on yourself if things don't go right – it's a short-lived influence!

JUNE: Main Trends: 1–2 Channel your great zest for life into brand new projects. 6–8 As Venus enters your sign, capitalise on this period of joy and great harmony with friends. This is a fine time to start new love affairs! 21–23 Focus on communication matters while they are favourably highlighted. This influence may also mean you are attracted to intellectual issues and may come up with an inventive

Please name FOULSHAM'S ALMANACK when replying to advertisers

Old Moore now Introduces you to Master Kuang and the Whispering Wisdom of your

CHINESE HOROSCOPE

EVERY DAY – IF YOU LIKE

Let Old Moore introduce you to his friend **Kuang C. Wang**. He is the great Chinese Master, whom Old Moore has invited to join his *personalised daily advice service*. By allowing Master Kuang the use of his new and massive computer, Old Moore can provide you with new, top quality Chinese guidance and wisdom thinking.

There is here a motivational thought for you every day.

Your daily rendezvous with Old Moore's friend, Kuang C. Wang will cost but a few pence per day* and you can hear this authoritative guide to your life, work and happiness. This is not the usual 'fortune telling' patter, but enlightened insights into how best to exploit your potential on any given day.

Unlike any other astro 'phone service, Master Kuang will be working from the day,

month and year of your birth to give you the most individual predictions at the lift of a 'phone. Ring this number and discover the most truly personalised advice.

Down the centuries, successful Chinese people have used the benefits of their ancient wisdom systems. In their daily living, they draw upon a cocktail of positive guidance. They use Astrology, Feng Shui, I-Ching and carefully selected *whispering thoughts of wisdom* to guide them for each coming day.

Yes, every day, the Chinese system combines its elements to produce thoughts of *wisdom*, which can help you to get the best out of any day.

Today there is such a thought for you. Your Guiding Principle for the day. And you can carry it through the day to help your intuitive powers. They can so greatly improve your life. And the decisions you make during the day.

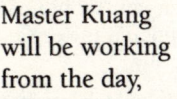

09068 805 493

*Calls cost 60p per minute at all times
Charges may be higher for payphones and non-BT networks

solution to a current matter. **Key Dates: Highs 19–20** Grasp any luck that is going to bring speedy success. **Lows 4–5** Beware of the downside to work as you may struggle with progress and accomplishment. Rest and gather your strength instead.

JULY: Main Trends: 4–5 A great period to involve yourself successfully in communication, meetings and appointments. **6–7** Make the most of this helpful influence concerning money issues. Look out for learning something useful whilst pursuing material issues. **22–23** Matters in the domestic sphere tend to be highly rewarding; look to your loved ones to make life comfortable. **Key Dates: Highs 16–17** To bring success, focus your sights on individual aims and rely on your instincts rather than others' advice. **Lows 1–3; 28–30** Be wary of making any big decisions under this influence.

AUGUST: Main Trends: 1–2 A period for being on the go and in the know. Look to communication issues for fulfilment, listening out for new information on the grapevine. **21–23** A good period for expressing yourself and drawing the crowds. Make the most of that ready-made audience and look to your love life for enjoyment. **27–28** A period of family rewards, so focus on the home and the past for all good things. **Key Dates: Highs 12–13** Capitalise on this positive influence for swift progress with any important plans. **Lows 25–26** It may be best to let others make major decisions and concentrate instead on short-term minor tasks.

SEPTEMBER: Main Trends: 18–19 A good time to put yourself about socially and be the centre of attention. With a little effort on your part, your love life should be highly rewarding. **23–24** Take full advantage of this favourable phase for your love life – socialise and enjoy yourself. **25–27** Seize the moment to further your potential in the practical world. Be prepared for work issues going your way and be ready to put the last touches to a plan, or to start anew. **Key Dates: Highs 8–10** Sheer luck may bring opportunities to get ahead. Be prepared to let your intuition guide you in the right direction. **Lows 21–22** Make the best of this phase when if something can go wrong, then it probably will!

OCTOBER: Main Trends: 10–11 Look out for a lucky break at work, which should bring some gratification. **16–17** Be prepared for minor tensions rising to the surface at home. Consider changing your surroundings and even a spot of DIY. **28–29** A favourable time for business transactions and for extending yourself socially, and possibly meeting someone new. **Key Dates: Highs 6–7** Take the opportunity to make fresh starts and put any promising ideas into operation. **Lows 19–20** Go with the flow and get some 'me time' during this phase.

NOVEMBER: Main Trends: 8–9 While your powers of attraction are at a maximum, focus on any social or romantic plans, which should prove favourable. **17–18** This is a great time to eliminate old situations that have deteriorated so you can make way for new ones – a transitional period. **22–24** Take advantage of this phase to begin constructive efforts for self-improvement or a general renovation of your life. Make the most too of the positive highlight on intimate partnerships. **Key Dates: Highs 2–3; 29–30** A time of inspiration, when you should concentrate on new projects or getting approval from others. **Lows 15–16** Your best option is to keep a low profile while your general energies may be lacking and you may be let down socially.

DECEMBER: Main Trends: 2–4 This is a phase in which to reap the benefits of emotional relationships and look to loved ones for support – you may even have to rely on them. **5–6** Widen your horizons and enhance your chances of success by taking a break or searching out some kind of intellectual or cultural improvement. **26–27** Use this trend to do something cultural or recreational with a love interest, especially outdoors. This is an auspicious time for embarking on a long journey. **Key Dates: Highs 1; 27–28** Be sure to benefit from these lucky days when the wheels of progress turn favourably. **Lows 12–14** Make the best you can of this time when progress may even come to a halt.

Please name FOULSHAM'S ALMANACK when replying to advertisers

THOUSANDS OF READERS REPORT

PEN & PAPER MAGIC REALLY WORKS!

P&P MAGIC FOR LOVE & LUST!

Ever since we first published *Pen & Paper (P&P) Magic* we have received a constant stream of testimonials from delighted readers. A few examples:

A clerk, frustrated by his colleague's behaviour, tries P&P magic. Two weeks later his colleague is moved to another department!

A woman, despairing that her boyfriend will never ring her tries P&P magic. He phoned the next day!

An elderly couple found their life made a misery when a 'problem family' moved in next door. They tried P&P magic: six weeks later the family were evicted!

A widow reports regular bingo & lottery wins! In six months several small lottery wins totalled £19,000 ($35,000)!

PEN & PAPER MAGIC IS THE ANSWER TO YOUR PRAYERS!

It is the answer because it is so simple! And so effective! Anyone can do it! **You can be sick in bed and do it!**
AND THE MAGIC INVOKED IS *POWERFUL!*
It is the same powerful magic employed by the wizards of old!
THE EXACT SAME SIGILS OF POWERFUL MAGIC USED BY THE WIZARDS OF OLD ARE HERE IN THIS BOOK!
Here is the book you've been waiting for, because it brings *real, powerful magic* in the simplest form!
AND YOU DON'T NEED INCENSES, CANDLES, OILS, ETC.! AND YOU *DON'T NEED TO* VISUALISE!
That's right – no struggling to form mental images!
It couldn't be simpler!

WHAT P&P MAGIC CAN DO FOR YOU

It can bring you romance ... it can make a person become your willing love slave (you think we're kidding? Just try it!) ... It can bring you money – seemingly out of thin air! ... It can make people want to give you money and presents ... And if you want to teach someone a lesson for doing you wrong it can exact revenge (but be careful; this stuff can be devastating).
THE SECRET LIES IN THE POWERFUL SIGILS & SYMBOLS IN THIS BOOK. All you have to do is draw them with pen & paper. *It doesn't matter if you are lousy at drawing or writing.* Accuracy and style are not important. *Just a rough replica of the sigils & symbols is all that is required.*
Ordinary pen & paper will do. You don't need any so-called 'magical ink'. You don't need any special pen or paper. Any pen or pencil or scrap of paper will do.

IT IS SO SIMPLE A CHILD CAN EVEN DO IT.

THE POWER BEHIND THIS BOOK

Over 50 years of magical experience lay behind this book. The authors, William Van & Kate Richardson, are life-long masters of the magical arts. They eschew mumbo jumbo, and *deliver true magic in a simple and practical way.*
NEVER HAVE WE SEEN MAGICAL INSTRUCTION PRESENTED SO CLEARLY AND SO SIMPLY. The authors have gone out of their way to make this magic as easy and accessible as possible. *Each page contains a complete start-to-finish P&P ritual:* absolutely everything you need to know is given in complete form on a single page – no cross-referencing of pages is required. No weeks of advanced training. You can get started the moment you receive this book.

HERE IS MAGIC YOU CAN PERFORM IMMEDIATELY!

If you have pen (or pencil) and paper you can start straight away. You can do it even if you are sick in bed. You can do it anywhere you find convenient.
The magic is genuine and powerful. There are no gimmicks in this book. No long words: just straight, practical information that a child can even follow.

Please send only £6.95 – made payable to 'Finbarr' – to: **Finbarr (OP)**, Folkestone, Kent CT20 2QQ. (Address is complete. The post code is unique to us. All mail orders must be to this address.) If you are in a hurry write 'PRIORITY' on face of envelope and add 75p for fast delivery. Overseas add £4 for air mail. Callers at Unit D, Concept Court, Shearway Business Park, Folkestone. Our catalogue of unusual mystic books 50p. *We have advertised in Old Moore's since 1975.* Please add YOUR name and address.

P&P MAGIC FOR JUSTICE & REVENGE!

FOCUSING YOUR THOUGHTS WITH PEN & PAPER IS A MAGICAL RITUAL IN ITSELF – AND WHEN IT IS DONE WITH THE POWERFUL SIGILS & SYMBOLS IN THIS BOOK *IT BECOMES AN IRRESISTIBLE FORCE FOR ACCOMPLISHING YOUR DESIRE!*
It is a force no man or woman can resist. Those in authority cannot resist. It works silently and invisibly through the vibrations of the Cosmos: *directly affecting the thoughts and emotions of those persons you target.*
One young lady who wrote to us is convinced that it was P&P that made her employer give her a much needed pay rise.
She also used it to win the affections of a man who had ignored her previously.
Such testimonials are typical of those received at our offices every day.
BUT YOU NEED TO TRY P&P MAGIC FOR YOURSELF TO BE CONVINCED – AND AMAZED.

Read This, If Nothing Else

Persons who have difficulty with writing or drawing need not worry. And those who find it hard to visualise need not worry either. *You need only pen (or pencil) and paper to draw rough images of the book's symbols.* You are not asked to be an artist. Whether you draw well or badly is not an issue. And as for the magic words of power you only have to copy them down as they appear.

AND REMEMBER – THERE IS NO VISUALISATION.

WHY P&P MAGIC WORKS

The ancient Egyptians believed that writing and drawing were magical acts. Only the priests and magicians could do this: the knowledge of writing and drawing was forbidden to the population as a whole. They believed that the gods' energies resided in symbols and images. *To draw these images with magical intent, they believed, was to invoke these divine energies.*
In Egypt, and elsewhere in the ancient world, men and women magicians were thought to add wealth and power to their already privileged position by their use of what the authors call 'pen and paper magic'.
YOUR INTENTIONS EXPRESSED THROUGH THE SYMBOLS AND MAGIC WORDS ON PAPER TAKE ON A LIFE OF THEIR OWN. THEY CAN THEN MANIFEST INTO REALITY – 'AS IF BY MAGIC'.
But there is no need for you to understand this. In order to have light you flick a light switch; you don't need to be an electrician. *Just follow the so-simple instructions in this book to make your fondest dreams come true!*

P&P MAGIC FOR FINANCIAL SUCCESS!

GET WHATEVER YOU WANT!

You will find the precise instructions you need for:
- GETTING THE LOVER YOU WANT (INCLUDING THE SAME SEX)!
- HOW TO GET A SECRET LOVE AND KEEP IT SECRET!
- HOW TO MAKE A PERSON LOVE YOU (AND WANT ONLY YOU)!
- HOW TO OBTAIN MONEY QUICKLY – WITHOUT WAITING!
- HOW TO UNEXPECTEDLY FIND MONEY!
- HOW TO GET A JOB OR A PROMOTION!
- HOW TO GET RICH AND WEALTHY!
- HOW TO OBTAIN JUSTICE!
- **HOW TO MAKE A NEIGHBOUR MOVE!**
- HOW TO PROTECT YOURSELF AGAINST TROUBLESOME PEOPLE!
- HOW TO DEFEND YOURSELF AGAINST A CURSE AND CURSE THE ONE WHO CURSED YOU!
- HOW TO EXACT REVENGE IN MONEY MATTERS!
- HOW TO REVENGE YOURSELF ON AN EX-LOVER!
- HOW TO REVENGE YOURSELF FOR ANY INJUSTICE!

These and many other rituals are outlined in the book, 'PEN & PAPER MAGIC'. IT IS YOUR IMMEDIATE OPPORTUNITY FOR SUCCESS.
Please send only £6.95.

GEMINI BORN PEOPLE
Birthdays: 22 May to 21 June inclusive
Planet: Mercury. Birthstone: Agate. Lucky day: Wednesday

Keynote for the Year: *A year for widening your cultural horizons in whatever way possible, while matters connected to the hearth and home may bring a new set of responsibilities.*

JANUARY: Main Trends: 3–4 Take advantage of this influence to advance your career goals and take any opportunity for self-determined success. **19–20** A time when you may just get the best of both worlds. Enjoy being out and about, talking with others. **21–22** Be prepared for well-meaning emotional support and enjoyable intimacies with a partner. This is the time to confide in those who mean the most to you. **Key Dates: Highs 8–9** Seize the moment and you should accomplish a great deal. Approach influential people for help if necessary. **Lows 21–22** You may encounter obstacles and should be prepared to chalk one or two things up to experience.

FEBRUARY: Main Trends: 2–3 A beneficial time for social get-togethers – get the most from existing friendships and newcomers. **4–5** Exercise diplomacy in dealings with those in authority – differences can arise from rigid opinions or a bolshie attitude. **20–22** Your prospects seem on the up and up. Make the most of your clever ideas for improving work methods and capitalising on current successes at work. **Key Dates: Highs 5–6** Expect practical endeavours to proceed smoothly and put forward new proposals as they should be accepted. **Lows 17–19** Pace yourself as there may be obstacles in the way of professional advancement and your vitality may be low.

MARCH: Main Trends: 8–9 Take advantage of this helpful period when certain important matters should be brought to a head. Whatever you are up to, it seems like a step in the right direction. **14–15** Beware of taking things too much for granted, as this may make business dealings difficult. **20–21** A time to take advantage of new social trends – be around others and enjoy their company as whoever you meet could have a positive effect on you. **Key Dates: Highs 3–4; 31** Look out for a personal plan of action receiving a major boost. This is also a safe period for risk taking. **Lows 16–18** Take care when it comes to personal schemes and your health.

APRIL: Main Trends: 12–13 Try to get a complete change of scenery while travel in particular and mental interests are favourably highlighted. **22–23** You may be handling all manner of demands from various people – don't overburden yourself and do have the courage to resist sometimes. **24–26** Professional matters should be more satisfying – take advantage of this, particularly when it comes to getting those in authority on your side. **Key Dates: Highs 1; 27–28** You may be looking and feeling good, and luck should bring personal or professional success. Make the most of it! **Lows 13–14** Tricky circumstances may make progress difficult. Be prepared to compromise or accept second best.

MAY: Main Trends: 13–15 Your imagination is stirred, but your thinking may not be as practical as usual. Ensure communications are not disorganised or unclear. **20–22** This influence may bring an energy boost and a more competitive edge. Even so, you shouldn't have to try too hard. **30–31** Be prepared for a lack of dynamism and energy. Don't get caught up negatively in the recent past. **Key Dates: Highs 24–25** Take advantage of this increase in personal vitality to make progress and get your own way. **Lows 10–12** Not the best time for ambitious ideas – other people may get what they want during this influence.

JUNE: Main Trends: 9–10 Don't expect emotional fulfilment or satisfaction in your love life – forbearance is the key. **14–15** Get out and see as much of life as possible as this should lift your spirits.

Lewis Hamilton

PA Photos

It's been a short road to success for the Formula One champion who began his incredible journey in a go-kart at the tender age of six. Lewis Carl David Hamilton was born on 7 January 1985, making him an ambitious Sun Capricorn with the Moon in sentimental Cancer. Capricorn often takes a long time to reach the top of its chosen mountain, but Lewis has been helped along by incredible talent and by lucky, expansive Jupiter that conjuncts his natal Sun. Capricorn is the sign of the archetypal father principle and Jupiter provides beneficial support – it is no surprise, then, that Hamilton senior went to enormous lengths to help his son during the early years.

Like a true pragmatic goat, Lewis has said that money is one of the reasons for his move to Switzerland. The other is to avoid the media glare – driven by his Moon (emotions) in Cancer, which makes him sensitive to the world around him and fosters a love of peace and quiet. He has a 'still waters run deep' quality and a vulnerable side, which may only be obvious to those who are close to him. He's emotionally responsive to partners (Moon opposite Jupiter) and his Piscean Venus conjoined with Mars bodes well for his love life.

Taskmaster Saturn in powerful Scorpio means Hamilton is emotionally reserved and guarded. He's said that he is trying to lead a normal life, though this is undoubtedly difficult, particularly with Saturn in hard aspect to the south node (relating to the public). A typical Capricorn, Hamilton believes in hard work and doesn't just rely on his good looks and agreeable manner. But pressures will mount as he struggles to remain in the mould of how everyone wants him to be.

The 'quiet hero' may chafe against his humble public image in 2009. As Pluto conjoins Neptune in January and July, there may be a time of soul-searching during which he looks again at certain goals and his desire to please others. In April, Uranus hits Mercury, bringing a frantic time of nervous energy when Lewis must avoid making rash decisions, especially in his professional life. One word of warning is very pertinent – one should always drive carefully with this influence as the danger of accidents (when on the move) is increased. In August, Neptune makes a harsh angle to Saturn, possibly leading to doubts over a personal matter and a desire to withdraw from any conflict. Finally, in late September, Jupiter contacts Saturn, bringing a tendency to try to take on all-comers and win. Rather than thinking himself invincible Hamilton should cut down on his commitments and try to simplify his life – this could well be an intense year.

Gemini: how to work with your good luck

Give in to the overriding desire to fulfil curiosities. **23–25** You should be in a better position to attract the good things of life. Capitalise on this and you may make gains in the money-making department. **Key Dates: Highs 21–22** You could be on a winning streak in your personal life. Concentrate on your goals and things may work in your favour. **Lows 6–8** There may be obstacles in your way, and you may struggle to find the energy to surmount them.

JULY: Main Trends: 2–3 Look to the outdoors, especially in the social world, to lift your spirits. **6–7** Grasp any opportunities in your love life while you have the knack for being popular and attractive to others. Make plans to get out and socialise. **22–24** A rather busy though quite interesting period, with many inspiring ideas in the air. Avoid scattering your energies on trivial matters. **Key Dates: Highs 18–19** Focus on professional developments while your luck is in. **Lows 4–5** The planetary picture is not really on your side – a time to hang fire and take life easy.

AUGUST: Main Trends: 1–3 Seek out opportunities for gain while money matters are positively highlighted – you may be on to a winner financially. **22–23** Your family life could bring reasons to celebrate. Focus on feeling closer to loved ones and spending quality time at home. **25–26** Be on the lookout for newcomers to the social scene, or invitations to spend time with friends. **Key Dates: Highs 14–16** Concentrate on putting new projects into action – the more ambitious you are the better. **Lows 1; 27–29** Your best option is to slow down and pace yourself.

SEPTEMBER: Main Trends: 18–19 Domestically a very fulfilling period so make the most of warm and affectionate encounters with others and happy new developments in your family life. **20–21** An influence that enhances pleasures at home and brings a sense of nostalgia, so take the time to relive the good old days and maybe call up an old friend. **26–27** Capitalise on your vitality and confidence to attract favourable attention. **Key Dates: Highs 11–12** Be sure to profit from your exciting and highly original thinking and sudden intuitive insights. **Lows 23–25** Your workload may be demanding and others may be over critical. Don't let your health suffer by doing too much – simplify your life.

OCTOBER: Main Trends: 10–12 Make sure that you're at the centre of things and get yourself noticed during this influence. Make the effort to go to places of leisure and entertainment too. **14–16** Let your light shine as creative and personal ambitions should be easier to achieve, and you can impress more than just social contacts. **23–24** The work situation is highlighted, so make the most of the helpful nature of colleagues and your superiors' approval for your plans. Put new ideas into practice. **Key Dates: Highs 8–9** Look to others for help with your plans as they should be only too glad to help. **Lows 21–22** Don't put pressure on yourself or others during this phase.

NOVEMBER: Main Trends: 8–9 A favourable period for practical affairs, so put changes into place and prepare for smoother progress in the long run. **15–16** Be open minded during this influence when you never know who you'll meet or who will have the information you're after. **23–24** Look to personal encounters for help on practical and emotional levels. Don't try going it alone. **Key Dates: Highs 4–5** A progressive time when much should go your way – look out for help even from unexpected sources. **Lows 17–19** Be prepared for setbacks and keep to the tried and tested path.

DECEMBER: Main Trends: 4–5 Look to social interactions for gleaning information, either directly or on the grapevine. **6–7** A favourable influence for finding ingenious solutions to practical problems. Trust your intuition to inform you about loved ones. **21–22** A personal dilemma may arise, so be prepared to take constructive action. Concentrate on clearing out the deadwood and getting ready to move on with new things. **Key Dates: Highs 2–3; 29–30** Your luck potential is strong, so go for it! **Lows 15–16** Unexpected changes can affect and disrupt your everyday life – beware of taking unnecessary risks in anything you're not sure of.

The Spoken Power

IT SAVES LIVES! IT PREVENTS INJURY! IT HEALS! IT HEALS RELATIONSHIPS! IT BRINGS MONEY! IT STOPS PAIN! STOPS FEVER!

Publisher James Finbarr writes –

For almost a quarter of a century I have had this secret in my file. It was an elderly Harold Jolet from Detroit who gave it to me, feeling it was safe in my hands. The problem was that he wanted me to publish it – and he didn't!

It was given to him by a man in the 1930s. Some 20 years earlier this man had used it when he witnessed two cars colliding before his very eyes. **Because of the Spoken Power, both drivers emerged unhurt, their vehicles miraculously unscathed!**

Mr Jolet believed this power could help anyone who respected it. His worry was that because it was originally kept secret, in the wrong hands it could be misused.

Hence his concern and my dilemma.

The Spoken Power consists of an 11-word sentence, in English, which releases awesome energy.

It can be spoken anywhere, any time. But only when needed!

Mr Jolet has since passed on, so the moral responsibility for publishing the Spoken Power became solely mine.

He recalled the time when lightning struck his neighbour's home, it catching fire. *He spoke the 11-word formula and the fire stopped.* Miraculously, there was no damage to the building!

Another time he ran to the scene of a car crash. The driver's nose was gushing blood. Mr Jolet spoke the miracle sentence and the bleeding *stopped immediately.* The driver was dumbfounded! Worst of all – in another incident involving a car – Mr Jolet wound up upside down after careering across a highway. *After speaking the Power his car immediately turned itself the right way up* … and he emerged without a scratch!

Over time, he revealed the secret to others – those he felt he could trust – to give them divine protection.

This is not a 'magickal formula' in the usual sense: the Spoken Power releases the divine *creative energy of the universe*.

A woman who received the secret from Mr Jolet – but who wishes not to be named – used it for her failing marriage. **Her husband was about to walk out when she spoke the Power. He changed his mind right there and then.**

Another time, her daughter was struck down by a mysterious illness. After speaking the Power, **she made an immediate recovery!** This same woman used the Spoken Power at the race track. **She won a bundle!**

Why does it work? Who knows? Mr Jolet explained to me what allegedly happened at the Creation. A different picture of God emerged! This I explain in the booklet.

Mr Jolet did not want this to be treated lightly. The Spoken Power is not for amusement.

Precisely because it is so simple, some people may fail to respect it. No previous experience – mystical or spiritual – is needed for the Spoken Power to work. All you need to know is in this booklet. DO NOT BE FOOLED BY ITS SIMPLICITY.

Can a miraculous divine power be immediately at hand when you most need it? Such a question many would ask. Now you can know; now you can ACTUALLY EXPERIENCE IT.

Only Finbarr would publish this. And even I have hesitated for almost a quarter of a century before doing so.

You do not have to belong to any secret society to possess true spiritual power – although this secret was originally known only to initiates. It is the spiritual gift of a lifetime.

In addition to the Spoken Power, there is a section in this booklet entitled 'Banishing Relationship Problems': how to *end once and for all, difficulties you may have with others*, be it a relative, lover, friend or colleague.

To receive, please send **£7.99**.

To order 'The Spoken Power' send £7.99 by cheque, postal order or cash, to: **Finbarr International (OSP), Folkestone, Kent CT20 2QQ**. Overseas send £9.99. Despatch within 7 days; but if you are in a hurry, add 75p and write 'PRIORITY' on face of envelope. Catalogue of unusual books, 50p. Callers can collect from Unit D, Concept Court, Shearway Business Park, Folkestone (9.00–5.00, Mon–Fri), but orders by mail must be sent to 'CT20 2QQ' address above.

Cancer: how to make the most of 2009

CANCER BORN PEOPLE
Birthdays: 22 June to 22 July inclusive
Planet: Moon. Birthstone: Ruby. Lucky day: Monday

Keynote for the Year: *Look to joint financial ventures for growth and expansion this year. Prepare for testing times in the sphere of travel and general communication.*

JANUARY: Main Trends: 3–4 Focus on pursuing personal interests. Opt for a change of scenery as travel and cultural matters are appealing during this phase. 19–20 If a recent project isn't working, it may be wise to abandon it, no matter how much you may want to hang on to it. 21–22 Make the most of this influence when your professional life is highlighted. Look to those who are well connected giving you their support as this can lead to job opportunities and promotions. **Key Dates: Highs 10–11** Capitalise on advantages that present themselves, and push forth with major plans. **Lows 23–25** Be prepared for minor frustrations and be patient when it comes to a career issue.

FEBRUARY: Main Trends: 3–4 Keep as high a profile as possible and listen out for news regarding a professional matter that you can later turn to good use. 5–6 Avoid relationships turning into power struggles – be prepared to compromise. Put your energies into clearing the decks for new action. 18–19 A great time to seek out the wide blue yonder and bring variety into your life. **Key Dates: Highs 6–7** Trust your instincts if you feel you are making the right moves. **Lows 20–21** Be prepared for some emotional pressure and be ready to give an issue the attention it requires.

MARCH: Main Trends: 8–10 Look out for opportunities to broaden your horizons – a change of scenery, or doing something new and interesting. 15–16 You may be more restless than usual. Consider long journeys and new environments as small changes may be insufficient. 21–22 Keep your eyes open for short cuts to success while those in authority are looking upon you favourably and seem more than willing to help. **Key Dates: Highs 5–7** Get an early start with important matters and make the most of your energy to accomplish things. **Lows 19–20** Don't expect everything to go according to plan. Be prepared to make some improvisational changes.

APRIL: Main Trends: 12–13 Take advantage of this influence to get rid of what is no longer essential. Make the most of loving support from partners, which may be material too. 19–20 Make this a time of happy socialising – get out there and make new contacts. 22–24 Unexpected career demands may detract from your personal desires as you set the world to rights – don't get too ambitious! **Key Dates: Highs 2–3; 29–30** Be sure to capitalise on this lucky phase. **Lows 15–17** Be prepared for certain aspects of daily life breaking down, and ensure that routines are properly co-ordinated.

MAY: Main Trends: 15–16 Focus on teamwork matters and listen out for invaluable information – possibly in social situations. 20–21 This planetary trend may see you rather vague and unfocused. Concentrate on solo pursuits and private matters and indulge your imagination! 30–31 Beware of asserting your own ideas and, though they may not be easy to make, consider compromises. **Key Dates: Highs 26–27** Capitalise on your greater self-confidence and resolve to assume a prominent and even lucky role at work. **Lows 13–14** Expect considerable demands on your time and energy and keep life as simple as possible.

JUNE: Main Trends: 6–7 Group matters tend to bring out the best in you so look to social contacts and friends for success. 14–15 Sit back and review your life progress. Concentrate on clearing up existing initiatives rather than concerning yourself with new ones. 21–22 Take centre stage while you have the power of personality to carry most things off. This is a time for new beginnings in just about

A need to move out of the shadows

Camilla, Duchess of Cornwall

PA Photos

Born on 17 July 1947 at 7am, Camilla has the Sun and Moon in sensitive Cancer and a Leo ascendant. Venus, the planet of love, is likewise in Cancer, bringing out her maternal qualities, while Mars is in Gemini, indicating an attraction to the cerebral and articulate, which she has found in her husband, Prince Charles.

Camilla's many years as the royal paramour were necessarily shrouded in secrecy, as indicated by the four major planets in the twelfth house (the subconscious). All of them are in Cancer, making her self-protective, emotional and secretive. This quota of introspective self-doubt and a feeling of being held back is a heavy placement, but unyielding Saturn and passionate Pluto in the first house have enabled her to be steadfast.

Pluto is in tense aspect to rumbustious Jupiter and gives us a clue to what Camilla really wants from life: power! Because of those concealed yet restrictive twelfth-house planets this can only be power behind the throne, but if she cannot wield influence outwardly, then she will use the art of subtle manipulation to get her own way. The planetoid Chiron (the mythic wounded healer) in hard aspect to the Leo ascendant (personality) again indicates the requirement to deny personal needs in the service of more influential personalities.

Neptune (often 'the cross one has to bear') on the fourth house cusp (family) suggests that there may be regret about not being able to bear the royal children, but supportive, providential Jupiter is also close by. Leo rising hints that Camilla may have a deep need for approval and respect – and even a share of the limelight.

Camilla's tough individuality and need to move out of the shadows and carve a more personal path may come to prominence in 2009. The major influences on her chart occur in January when personal relationships and/or social contacts may help to further her life progress. This expansive, even lucky Jupiterian influence forms a background for the year, enabling her to do far more of her own thing. But Jupiter's clashes with Saturn and Pluto in February are a warning not to expect too much from others. March sees a major progression by Mercury to Neptune and whilst some ideas and decisions may be confused, her imagination and creativity is let loose. As the progressed Mercury (communication) moves to the fourth house cusp in September there may be a powerful emphasis on the past and personal or family history – prompting a book or a TV documentary, perhaps. Creativity and fulfilment are also augmented by solar progressions in November and December which may put Camilla in the public eye more than previously. A slow process seems to be under way towards gaining public acceptance and maybe even admiration!

Cancer: a guide to your lucky days

any area. **Key Dates: Highs 23–24** You should be able to get others to agree to your requests, so capitalise on this to make your own luck. **Lows 9–10** Progress may be slow so be prepared to adapt to the circumstances – either roll with the punches or put off important matters until later.

JULY: Main Trends: 3–4 Daily circumstances should keep you busy but interested too – use your more versatile side. **4–5** Relationships may bring an emotional dip and you may not be able to depend on the right response. Try to keep things realistic, and if there's something bothering a loved one, try to find out what it is. **22–24** Focus on the physical side of life by working and playing hard. Prepare too for a time of financial consolidation when recent plans are at stake. **Key Dates: Highs 20–21** Capitalise on this trend to get matters up and running. Make the most of the good fortune that may be on its way. **Lows 6–8** Obstacles may be hard to handle – keep life simple or things could get too much!

AUGUST: Main Trends: 1–3 Take advantage of your outgoing nature to bring romantic or social enjoyment. This could be a great time for entertaining others or even starting new affairs. **22–23** A breezy phase when avenues of communication may open up – look to encounters with others to keep abreast of interesting news. **26–27** Finances are highlighted, so make the most of your luck and look out for life's little luxuries. **Key Dates: Highs 17–18** Little stands in the way of progress, so capitalise on this to do some business. **Lows 2–4; 30–31** Don't worry too much about progressing with major ambitions – take a rest between such activities.

SEPTEMBER: Main Trends: 18–19 A mental peak when your judgement should prove pretty sound, so don't be afraid to make quick decisions. **20–21** A little mental refreshment is probably all you need. Be ready for a new experience and bear in mind that conversations could be productive. **22–23** A sense of nostalgia may be in the air, so focus on issues at home to make life feel comfortable, and look to loved ones for help. **Key Dates: Highs 13–14** The more open you are to new ideas the better – expect the best from life and it may just happen. **Lows 26–27** Not your luckiest time – be prepared for personal disappointment and get lots of rest.

OCTOBER: Main Trends: 12–13 The atmosphere at home should make life seem interesting. Consider making improvements during this busy period. **16–17** Avoid the spendthrift tendencies that come with this trend, and try instead to be careful and sensible. **28–30** This is not a time to hide your light under a bushel! Put your creative talents to use and get out to places of leisure and entertainment. **Key Dates: Highs 10–11** Enhance your chances of success by using your considerable optimism and energy, and your generally dynamic nature. **Lows 23–25** Sideline ambitious ideas during this phase – sit back and relax instead.

NOVEMBER: Main Trends: 8–9 Enjoy an improved social and romantic lifestyle and capitalise on your considerable charm. **16–17** Make the most of your good ideas for improving work routines and alternative ways of making progress. **22–24** Be prepared for satisfactory results at work and look to the co-operation of others to bring fulfilment. **Key Dates: Highs 6–7** Take advantage of this beneficial phase to bring personal and professional advancement. **Lows 20–21** A career issue may prove rather tricky – put off important decisions for a while.

DECEMBER: Main Trends: 1–2 Practical issues should progress smoothly, but you should avoid being too laissez-faire as this could lead to sloppy results. **6–7** Make this a fulfilling period socially by focusing on encounters with others – these should be informative and enlivening. **21–22** Take advantage of potential happy times in your relationships and love life. Keep up a high profile as this may lead to some fortunate contacts. **Key Dates: Highs 17–18** Positive thinking can work wonders – capitalise on your increased vigour to get things done. **Lows 4–5; 31** There may be no quick fixes for everyday problems. Your best option may be to rest and leave things until later.

THE TEN DAY 'MONEY MIRACLE' TECHNIQUE
Receive the money you seek within days.

IT DOESN'T MATTER HOW DESPERATE YOUR SITUATION – THIS POWERFUL TECHNIQUE WILL HELP YOU. IT DOESN'T MATTER IF YOU HAVE NO JOB, NOR ANY MEANS OF RAISING CASH – ALL YOU NEED IS THE BELIEF THAT THIS AMAZING OCCULT TECHNIQUE WILL WORK FOR YOU.

Jason Pike, author of this new book, believed. He was once penniless and faced disastrous consequences if he could not raise the £500 needed to pay off a loanshark within 14 days. He had no income and no earthly chance, it seemed, of getting the money. But he believed in the powers of the occult and suddenly one evening he discovered something that could help him. Within four days a friend he hadn't seen in years appeared out of the blue and gave him £800.

THIS ACTUALLY HAPPENED, and such 'money miracles' happen time and time again for those who believe.

WHATEVER YOU NEED FINANCIALLY YOU CAN NOW RECEIVE. It usually takes ten days for the money to appear, although sometimes much less.

Mr Pike's technique is based on moral, karmic principles. It is not black magick. It is safe and simple. Mr Pike is a Christian occultist and eschews any abuse of occult powers.

This technique can be used by Muslim, Jew, Christian – who ever. Poverty is a sin in God's eyes, no matter what your religion, according to Mr Pike, and even if you belong to no religion at all it doesn't matter – it only matters that you believe in the principle of Cosmic supply.

Use his technique for ten days and you will be amazed!

But there is more – he also reveals one of the great money prosperity formulae of the ancient Egyptians. Another bonus is the mantric word of power 'Feyou' which can ensure *that you will never lack for money again.*

Please send **£5.50** to: **Finbarr (O/10), Folkestone, Kent CT20 2QQ.** Overseas £8.
If in a hurry write 'PRIORITY' on envelope for fast delivery. Catalogue of unusual books 50p. PLEASE GIVE NAME & ADDRESS!

NEW SALT MAGICK RITES

Chapters include: **Salt Magick Brings Money – Influencing Another Person's Thoughts & Actions – Salt Rites To Protect Against Physical Injury – Salt Rite To Get A Job.** Are you aware that sprinkling salt outside your front door could keep unwanted persons away? Everything explained in this volume. Also details for sprinkling salt on important documents and lottery coupons. Common table salt from your supermarket is all you need. Note these unsolicited testimonials (copies of originals available on request): 'Have already had two wins on the pools' (M.B., Fleetwood); 'In ten minutes my violent son quietened down ... have had no trouble from him since' (P.E., Manchester); 'IT REALLY WORKS! I won £1411' (A.P., Grimsby); 'Since I got your book ... money has come into my home in different ways ... my son has paid off his debts ... I bless the day I sent for this book' (D.I., Hove – this same lady wrote again five months later: 'The salt rites are still working for us ... every day we receive something good!'). To receive 'New Salt Magick Rites' please send **£4.99** to: **Finbarr (OS), Folkestone, Kent CT20 2QQ** (address complete). Overseas send £7.50.

HOW TO FIND YOUR TRUE SOUL MATE

Everyone has a true soul mate – but how does one find him/her out of the billions on this planet? Booklet reveals miraculous solution! Please send **£3.99** to **Finbarr (OSM), Folkestone, Kent CT20 2QQ.** Overseas £6.

---

20 POWERFUL VOODOO RITES FOR FAST CASH

Twenty voodoo rites dealing exclusively with raising money! Information for shopkeepers, stockbrokers, salespeople, business people – anyone engaged in making money. Also for the average person: HOW TO ENJOY WINNING STREAKS IN GAMBLING ... RECEIVE CASH AND GIFTS ... AND MORE! Please send **£7.99** to: **Finbarr (OV), Folkestone, Kent CT20 2QQ.** Overseas £11.

MASTER WORDS OF MYSTIC POWER

Revolutionary mind power methods! Devised and tested by psychologist Veronica Reade, THEY WORK INSTANTANEOUSLY! BE IMMEDIATELY CONFIDENT! ... BE ABSOLUTELY CALM IN STRESSFUL SITUATIONS! ... IMMEDIATELY CONCENTRATE PERFECTLY! ... ACTIVATE – IN A FLASH – YOUR ARTISTIC TALENTS: BECOME CREATIVE AND INSPIRED WITHIN MOMENTS! – STOP PEOPLE USING YOU! ... DEVELOP WILL POWER ... SUCCEED IN SLIMMING! ... CONTROL UNRULY PERSONS – EVEN ANIMALS! ... ERASE GUILT FEELINGS! ... FREE YOURSELF OF WORRY! ... FIND A LOST OBJECT! ... FIND TRUE LOVE! ... STOP BAD LUCK! The possibilities are amazing and endless with these proven methods! To receive this amazing book please send **£7.99** to: **Finbarr (OM), Folkestone, Kent CT20 2QQ** (address complete). Overseas £11.

HOW TO LOOK INCREDIBLY YOUNG/ HOW TO BECOME TALLER

Potent psychological techniques for looking 10 ... 20 years younger! Also a unique exercise for increasing height by 1½". Please send **£4.99** to **Finbarr (OY), Folkestone, Kent CT20 2QQ.** Overseas £7.

THE NEW AUTO-SUGGESTION:
The New, Easy Way to Release the Wondrous Powers of Your Subconscious Mind

Simple psychological technique! Within minutes learn to: LOSE WEIGHT! ... IMPROVE HEALTH! ... FIND A LOVER! ... STOP BAD HABITS! ... END INSOMNIA! ... BANISH CLAUSTROPHOBIA and AGROPHOBIA! ... IMPROVE MEMORY! ... GET OTHERS TO SEE YOUR POINT OF VIEW! ... RECEIVE MONEY! ... and much, much more! Please send **£3.99** to: **Finbarr (OA), Folkestone, Kent CT20 2Q.** Overseas £6.

LEO BORN PEOPLE
Birthdays: 23 July to 23 August inclusive
Planet: Sun. **Birthstone:** Sapphire. **Lucky day:** Sunday

Keynote for the Year: *Make the most of potential gains in one-to-one relationships while keeping an eye on financial changes and challenges, especially in your personal budget.*

JANUARY: Main Trends: 3–5 A time when you can make improvements to a current relationship – a tête-à-tête may help put a new perspective on things. **19–20** Make the most of this influence as it may boost chances for new romance and whatever does begin around now may prove highly significant. **21–22** This is the time to emphasise the practical side of life, clearing up as many outstanding minor tasks as you can. **Key Dates: Highs 12–13** Seize the opportunity to put new and ambitious ideas into practice. **Lows 26–27** It may now feel as if little is going right – don't be surprised if personal plans are held up.

FEBRUARY: Main Trends: 3–4 Grab every opportunity to get outside and enjoy the outdoor life. Make the most of an easier time at work and feeling more relaxed generally. **5–6** You're not really in a compromising mood, so going solo may be a better option than social encounters. **18–19** Take advantage of this good period for sharing emotional issues with a partner, and life may be more peaceful as a result. **Key Dates: Highs 8–9** Put your excellent persuasive powers to the test – coercion should work well in just about any situation. **Lows 22–24** There could be minor setbacks ahead, so take it easy.

MARCH: Main Trends: 10–11 This phase may help clear your mind and get you ready to tackle problems, so have a clean out, revitalise things and make way for new experiences. **15–16** Make the most of your accurate intuition and your ability to influence others. **19–20** You should enjoy a challenge, and will thrive anywhere that gives you an opportunity to expand your horizons – travel could be an option. **Key Dates: Highs 8–9** While your enthusiasms and will power are strong, make the effort to get your own way. **Lows 21–23** You may lack confidence where its most needed, so consider keeping a low profile.

APRIL: Main Trends: 12–13 Your love life is highlighted – make the most of being forthright in expressing your feelings and being a lively presence socially. **22–23** Enjoy any mental stimulation, but while you can be very persuasive, beware a tendency to browbeat others! **24–25** Take any opportunities to discuss issues and get important messages across. A great time for travelling with a partner – the further the better! **Key Dates: Highs 4–5** Enhance your chances of success by eliciting the help of those who really matter to your plans. **Lows 18–19** Certain things may stand in your way, so salvage what you can from any no-win situations and start again if necessary.

MAY: Main Trends: 13–14 Career-wise there is very little you can't accomplish once you set your mind to it. A superb time to put new ideas into practice and to get others on side. **20–21** Focus on teamwork and group issues while social developments are making life feel comfortable. **30–31** Steer clear of any run-ins with those in authority as you may not want to acknowledge a 'higher power' in your quest to fulfil your ambitions! **Key Dates: Highs 1–2; 28–29** Put your faith in your intuition when it comes to major decision-making. **Lows 15–16** This mid-month lull may put you to the test – don't expect too much from life.

JUNE: Main Trends: 6–8 Your professional life may experience a boost. Look to help from those in authority to bring success. **14–16** You have a talent for making friendships and function well in a team – a great time for joining a group! **21–22** A change of pace makes this is an excellent time to take it

Something new to wow us?

Ant and Dec

PA Photos

This irrepressible pair of 'Likely Lads' from Newcastle have been around so long that it is sometimes hard to believe that they are both still in their early thirties. Ant (Anthony McPartlin) was born on 18 November 1975, and Dec (Declan Donnelly) was born on 25 September 1975. This makes Ant a steamy Scorpio, though with lots of positively placed planets in his natal chart, and Dec an easy-going Libran. Fortunately they share a great deal astrologically providing strong points of reference. Any severe fallout is extremely unlikely – if this were a romantic attachment it might be referred to as a marriage made in heaven! Their relationship works because the negatives in one chart are balanced out by the positives in the other.

Their friendship started on the set of the kids' television soap *Byker Grove*, way back in 1990. They then enjoyed a successful musical career, using their *Byker Grove* character names, PJ and Duncan, before climbing the rungs of stardom as TV presenters. For a while it looked as though their careers were on the wane when in 1998 the BBC let them go, but ITV signed them for Saturday morning TV and an evening extravaganza followed, with shows such as *Pop Idol*, *PokerFace* and *I'm a Celebrity... Get Me Out of Here!*

It might seem as if there isn't anywhere else for this award-winning pair to go, but nothing could be further from the truth. *I'm a Celebrity* looks like running and running, and indications from both birth charts are that by 2009 the pair will dream up something entirely new that will once again take the nation by storm. With Dec's love of the film industry, another Ant and Dec movie is likely, and some solo work may also be in the offing, though the fact that each has the other's life insured for a sizeable sum says a great deal about their commitment to the partnership.

Dec, with four Air sign planets in his chart is always going to be the more optimistic of the two. Ant's chart is filled with fire and water, which makes him more reactive and inclines him to darker thoughts than his Libran buddy. We know them for their zany humour and 'boy next door' appeal, but they are also shrewd and possess great stamina, a good business sense and a realistic approach to life.

Both have solid family values and a passion for Newcastle United football team that verges on obsession. They are level-headed and likeable – a fact that isn't lost on audiences in Britain and well beyond. But despite the fact that we can expect a definite flirt with America in the near future, Ant and Dec are a home-grown phenomenon and are likely to be enlivening our Saturday nights for many years to come.

Leo: tune into your good-luck times

easy and reflect on your life. **Key Dates: Highs** 25–26 Capitalise on the fact that moves made during this phase should turn out just as planned. **Lows** 11–13 Life may drag and expecting too much may lead to disappointments. Make the best of this period when enthusiasms may be running low.

JULY: Main Trends: 3–4 Be prepared for daily issues proving tiresome and a lack of patience when it comes to certain initiatives. 5–6 Capitalise on your personal charm and sociability – others should bring out the best in you. 24–25 Energy levels are good so use this period to burn the candle at both ends and to make your own opportunities. **Key Dates: Highs** 22–23 Make the most of this phase during which current endeavours should move swiftly towards target and you should be at the forefront of recent developments. **Lows** 9–10 Decisions based on instinct could prove wrong, so put certain plans on ice and get on with something less taxing.

AUGUST: Main Trends: 3–4 Be aware that your control over life may lessen and overtures to others may fall flat. Try to be patient in your love life! 7–8 Financial fortunes seem to be pretty good – capitalise on your firm position when it comes to making plans for short-term security. 26–27 You will love being the centre of attraction, so make the most of your ability to draw others towards you and gain new admirers. **Key Dates: Highs** 19–20 Take advantage of the fact that luck is on your side. **Lows** 5–6 It may be hard to find support for your ideas, and arguments may arise with those who oppose your way of thinking.

SEPTEMBER: Main Trends: 18–19 There is the potential for financial luck, possibly via the help of a partner. If you're ready to take risks, cash concerns can be highly lucrative. 20–21 Economic issues remain favourably highlighted – keep your eyes and ears open for new opportunities and focus on negotiations too. 23–24 An excellent time for talking, expressing your ideas and making short journeys. **Key Dates: Highs** 15–16 Be prepared to burn the midnight oil when it comes to work and make the most of your luck potential. **Lows:** 1; 28–30 Your ideas may not be the most practical and maintaining progress may not be worth all the effort it takes.

OCTOBER: Main Trends: 10–11 Make the most of your ability to charm others and express yourself in a crowd – engage in discussions or negotiations. 14–15 Everyday life should be running smoothly. This is a good period for gathering useful information that relates to recent endeavours. 23–24 Look to friends or family for enjoyment. Don't be afraid to elicit the help of others with any minor problems. **Key Dates: Highs** 12–13 Capitalise on your knack for finding assistance with either personal or professional moves. **Lows** 26–27 Circumstances may prove demanding and your energy levels low, so take things easy.

NOVEMBER: Main Trends: 8–9 Focus on issues around the hearth and home. A family member with your best interests at heart may do something heart-warming for you. 16–17 You may find yourself in the limelight, so make the most of your ability to entertain the crowd. 24–26 Your romantic prospects are looking good – make a little effort and you should be able to attract just the right people! **Key Dates: Highs** 8–10 Concentrate on career decisions while you are gifted and lucky in this area. **Lows** 22–24 You are likely to lack self-discipline, so it's best to take things slowly.

DECEMBER: Main Trends: 1–2 Romance is highlighted – make the most of being more in tune with your own needs and those of loved ones. 4–5 Concentrate on rising to life's challenges and your career objectives may well see favourable progress. 17–18 Capitalise on your popularity and a degree of good will to bring professional advancement. **Key Dates: Highs** 6–7 You should find it easy to make an impact on others, so undertake ambitious personal projects and try out your luck. **Lows** 19–21 Beware of getting hold of the wrong end of the stick in communications – it might be best to maintain a low profile.

THE SECRETS OF FINGER MAGIC

Perhaps no other magic is as old – or as simple – as FINGER or HAND magic. Yet its uses are almost unknown today.

Everyone is aware of the superstition 'Keep your fingers crossed for good luck', and the well known two fingers for victory, not to mention impolite finger gestures! But few are aware of the *hidden meaning* of hand gestures and their *magical significance*.

'Within a week of using it I have a beautiful new girlfriend … my bank balance is increasing', wrote A.H. of Stockport. **'Had great success'** (N.W., Dorking). These are typical comments. (Copies of actual letters on request.)

You can now get ready to enjoy this oldest and simplest of magical formulae!

THERE IS NO OTHER LIKE IT!

It is the secret magic of Adepts, applied to everyday situations, when there is no time nor place for formal ritual!

J.Y. (Cork) was anxious about her boyfriend's plight. Whilst in court she made the appropriate magical hand gestures, though the chances of success seemed non-existent.

To her joy he was acquitted!

'I never told anyone what I did, for no one would have believed me', she wrote, 'but I am convinced it was because of this, because so many other amazing things happened since I bought the book.'

Each finger corresponds to a magical elemental and zodiacal type: gestures correspond to defined unconscious impulses. It is these impulses which create the 'magic', declares author I. Curry!

M.F. (Brighton) wrote that **she won at bingo six straight weeks** after reading the monograph!

P.C. (Limerick) wrote that his **migraine attack stopped within minutes**. He wrote further that his migraine attacks are now much less frequent, but 'that when they do occur I am not worried – I know what to do!'

FINGER MAGIC CAN BE DONE ANYTIME, ANYWHERE! No rituals! No candles! No herbs! 'No nothing!' as one man (J.S., Edmonton) eloquently wrote! 'I couldn't believe anything could come of something so easy … I felt silly, but what the heck – I had nothing to lose. I wanted this loan so badly, and I was convinced I didn't stand a ghost of a chance. The man couldn't see how I had my fingers placed.'

'You could have knocked me down with a feather when he said I could have the money immediately – no problem!'

Once you get this monograph you have nothing else to buy. You can learn to apply Finger Magic within minutes.

'I have no problems getting girls', wrote a young man, P.W. (Dublin). 'Since I have been using it not one has said "no". I use it daily for so many other things too! I now use Finger Magic on a daily basis automatically and without thinking. It's the best thing ever to happen to me.'

Miss Curry, an advanced magician in a secret Irish lodge, claims specifically that Finger Magic can:
(A) GET YOU A NEW CAR
(B) BRING LUXURY GOODS
(C) GET YOU A PAY INCREASE – EVEN AGAINST THE ODDS!
(D) WIN LOTTERIES
(E) WINS AT THE RACETRACK
(F) MONEY TO PAY BILLS AND SETTLE DEBTS
(G) RAISE CASH TO BUY A HOUSE

Moreover it can be applied to all kinds of health problems, she says. Such as: **healing a wound … losing weight … curing a hangover(!) … curing illness … healing a friend … healing animals.**

Finger Magic can, she says, **arouse sexual passion (it can also be used to DECREASE it) … attract the person you want … turn an enemy into a friend … make someone change their mind … control unruly children.**

You can even **ease a guilty conscience**, she says. You can: **gain peace of mind … end a family feud … end insomnia … stop people quarrelling … make yourself calm and contented … meet the perfect mate … get promotion at work.**

Finger Magic can even BRING YOU A PERFECT FIGURE, says Miss Curry. You can stop smoking. It can give you INSPIRATION for CREATIVE projects. It can make you clairvoyant.

Finger Magic is perfectly safe. No evil spirits are conjured. It works for good, she says, BUT – IT CAN BE APPLIED TO DIFFICULT PEOPLE: not to harm them, but to leave you alone.

It can, she says, MAKE AN UNWANTED LOVER OR SPOUSE GO AWAY.

It can be used to stop gossip and slander.

IT CAN MAKE A DIFFICULT NEIGHBOUR MOVE.

'My life was a misery,' wrote J.G. (Hackney), 'I had to sleep in the daytime, but the confounded woman upstairs would play her loud music continuously. I complained, but all I got from her was "It's a free world, mate!", then she would play it even louder. I was driven to distraction, for not only was I not getting any sleep, my nerves were bad and my concentration poor. My health and my job were on the line because of this dreadful, uncaring person.

'I sent for your book, but frankly I was not optimistic. How could something this easy have any effect? Anyway, I was flabbergasted when only a week later I saw a removal van turn up – my horrible neighbour was actually going!'

With Finger Magic you can **overcome shyness … attract friends … get the person of your dreams … become successful in your chosen field.** Miss Curry explains it all.

For many people Finger Magic is a Godsend, for not everyone has the time or privacy to practise formal ritual. And some live with people who do not approve of such things – to be caught performing magic ritual in some households can be most embarrassing, or worse!

This is discreet … easy … simple. Nobody need know. You can learn it within minutes.

Whether you are an experienced occultist or a complete newcomer **nobody can afford to be without Finger Magic. Only £5.**

Please send cheque or postal order for £5 – made payable to 'Finbarr' – to: **Finbarr (OF), Folkestone, Kent CT20 2QQ.** (Address is complete. The post code is unique to us). All mail orders must be to this address. If you are in a hurry write 'PRIORITY' on the face of the envelope and add 75p for fast delivery. Overseas add £4 for air mail. Please include YOUR name and address. Callers at Unit D, Concept Court, Shearway Business Park, Folkestone. Our catalogue of unusual mystic books 50p. *We have advertised in Old Moore's since 1975.*

More power to the Silver Surfers

'I promise you – it's easy. I will bring the world to your armchair.'

978-0-572-03125-1 £6.99

978-0-572-03234-0 £7.99

978-0-572-032310-1 £7.99

978-0-572-03367-5 £8.99

These straightforward **step-by-step** guides will look after you right from square one. With **full-colour** screenshots every step of the way and **practical projects** to show you just how useful the **internet** can be, they will give you the **confidence** you can only gain from **success**.

978-0-572-03447-4 £8.99

To order, phone MDL on 01256 302699
or visit our website www.foulsham.com
(plus p+p)

36

JANUARY

For High Water add 5h 30m for Bristol, 4h 23m for Hull, 0h 43m for Leith; subtract 2h 21m for Dublin, 1h 26m for Greenock, 2h 29m for Liverpool.

D of M	D of W	Festivals and Special Events for 2009	Sun at London Rises	Sun at London Sets	High Water at London Bridge am	High Water at London Bridge pm	Moon at London Rises	Moon at London Sets	Weather
			h m	h m	h m	h m	h m	h m	
1	Th	New Year's Day	08 06	16 02	04 22	16 53	10 18	21 33	Belts of rain will affect all parts during the first fortnight, with local flooding in the Midlands and north. Winds will often be strong. A colder, drier spell will follow, but the last week will be stormy.
2	F	Scottish Bank Holiday	08 06	16 03	04 55	17 28	10 31	22 46	
3	Sa	Alaska became US state 1959	08 06	16 05	05 27	18 06	10 43	—	
4	Su	Louis Braille b. 1809	08 06	16 06	06 04	18 50	10 57	00 02	
5	M	Theodore Roosevelt d. 1919	08 05	16 07	06 50	19 46	11 14	01 21	
6	Tu	Epiphany	08 05	16 08	07 52	21 01	11 35	02 45	
7	W	Emperor Hirohito d. 1989	08 04	16 09	09 18	22 17	12 06	04 11	
8	Th	Kegworth plane crash 1989	08 04	16 11	10 36	23 27	12 50	05 36	
9	F	Tommy Handley d. 1949	08 03	16 12	11 49	—	13 54	06 50	
10	Sa	George Foreman b. 1949	08 03	16 14	00 30	12 56	15 15	07 47	
11	Su	Richmal Crompton d. 1969	08 02	16 15	01 26	13 50	16 47	08 27	
12	M	P.W. Botha b. 1926	08 02	16 16	02 16	14 41	18 19	08 54	
13	Tu	Wyatt Earp d. 1929	08 01	16 18	03 02	15 29	19 48	09 14	
14	W	First Gallup poll 1937	08 00	16 19	03 47	16 15	21 11	09 30	
15	Th	Elizabeth I crowned 1559	07 59	16 21	04 31	17 00	22 31	09 45	
16	F	British Museum opened 1759	07 58	16 22	05 11	17 42	23 49	09 58	
17	Sa	Al Capone b. 1899	07 57	16 24	05 54	18 26	—	10 12	
18	Su	Scott at South Pole 1912	07 56	16 26	06 36	19 12	01 04	10 28	
19	M	Edgar Allen Poe b. 1809	07 55	16 27	07 26	20 06	02 19	10 48	
20	Tu	David Garrick d. 1779	07 54	16 29	08 28	21 08	03 32	11 14	
21	W	Cecil B. de Mille d. 1959	07 53	16 31	09 43	22 22	04 39	11 48	
22	Th	Mike Hawthorn d. 1959	07 52	16 32	11 10	23 37	05 39	12 32	
23	F	Salvador Dali d. 1989	07 51	16 34	—	12 12	06 28	13 28	
24	Sa	Ann Todd b. 1909	07 50	16 36	00 30	13 00	07 06	14 33	
25	Su	Burns Night (Burns b. 1759)	07 48	16 37	01 12	13 39	07 34	15 43	
26	M	Chinese New Year festival	07 47	16 39	01 49	14 16	07 55	16 56	
27	Tu	Holocaust Memorial Day	07 46	16 41	02 24	14 49	08 12	18 10	
28	W	W.B. Yeats d. 1939	07 44	16 43	02 59	15 25	08 27	19 23	
29	Th	W.C. Fields d. 1879	07 43	16 44	03 33	15 58	08 39	20 36	
30	F	Charles I beheaded 1649	07 41	16 46	04 04	16 31	08 52	21 51	
31	Sa	Jean Simmons b. 1929	07 40	16 48	04 34	17 03	09 05	23 08	

MOON'S PHASES JANUARY 2009		Days	Hours	Mins
☽	First Quarter	4	11	56
○	Full Moon	11	3	27
☾	Last Quarter	18	2	46
●	New Moon	26	7	55

All times on this page are GMT

PREDICTIONS

The *Full Moon* on 11 January falls in Cancer in a harmonious aspect to Saturn and Uranus, and in a conjunction with the Sun in the United Kingdom chart. This bodes well for a positive start to the year and a sense that anything is possible. However, plans for a new generation of nuclear power plants could run into serious safety issues, perhaps as a result of an accident that could occur either in the UK or in Pakistan. There may also be news of Green initiatives, including plans to extract heat from the earth's core. There should be good news about the housing market with relief on the way for homeowners. Easier credit and lower interest rates are likely.

The *New Moon* on 26 January is an eclipse of the Sun and falls in Cancer in an exact conjunction with Jupiter. There could be terrorist panics in the UK, with fears of potential attacks on the transport and communication system, including computer networks. Siberia and Southeast Asia are additional areas of concern. This is a crucial moment for China, which opens the year in an aggressive mood and will be putting pressure on Taiwan with calls for Chinese reunification. International tension is likely to be high as a result.

At National Hunt meetings this month, favourites in the novice chases may do better than those taking part in hurdle races.

Predicted a crash in the property market, 2008

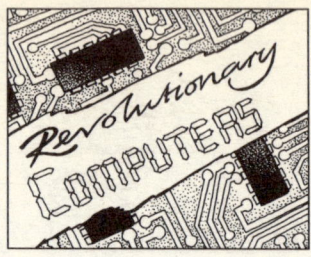

FEBRUARY

For High Water add 5h 30m for Bristol, 4h 23m for Hull, 0h 43m for Leith; subtract 2h 21m for Dublin, 1h 26m for Greenock, 2h 29m for Liverpool.

D of M	D of W	Festivals and Special Events for 2009	Sun at London Rises	Sun at London Sets	High Water at London Bridge am	High Water at London Bridge pm	Moon at London Rises	Moon at London Sets	Weather
1	Su	Dame Clara Butt b. 1873	07 38	16 50	05 04	17 38	09 20	—	Generally a mild, wet month. There is, however, a risk of gales in all areas during the first three weeks. Thereafter the weather will be drier, increasingly sunny and mild, and less windy.
2	M	Buddy Holly d. 1959	07 37	16 52	05 38	18 16	09 39	00 28	
3	Tu	Felix Mendelssohn b. 1809	07 35	16 53	06 19	19 05	10 05	01 51	
4	W	Guatemala earthquake 1976	07 33	16 55	07 15	20 16	10 41	03 15	
5	Th	First BBC 'pips' 1926	07 32	16 57	08 44	21 43	11 34	04 31	
6	F	Sky TV service launch 1989	07 30	16 59	10 15	23 06	12 45	05 34	
7	Sa	Dora Bryan b. 1924	07 28	17 01	11 41	—	14 10	06 20	
8	Su	Boeing 747 first flew 1969	07 27	17 03	00 18	12 49	15 41	06 52	
9	M	Carmen Miranda b. 1909	07 25	17 04	01 15	13 43	17 12	07 16	
10	Tu	Sophie Tucker d. 1966	07 23	17 06	02 04	14 31	18 39	07 34	
11	W	Vatican City established 1929	07 21	17 08	02 48	15 15	20 03	07 49	
12	Th	Charles Darwin b. 1809	07 19	17 10	03 29	15 56	21 24	08 03	
13	F	William & Mary access. 1689	07 17	17 12	04 07	16 35	22 43	08 17	
14	Sa	St Valentine's Day	07 16	17 13	04 45	17 11	—	08 33	
15	Su	Graham Hill b. 1929	07 14	17 15	05 21	17 48	00 00	08 52	
16	M	Castro premier of Cuba 1959	07 12	17 17	05 59	18 26	01 15	09 15	
17	Tu	Geronimo d. 1909	07 10	17 19	06 43	19 11	02 26	09 46	
18	W	Len Deighton b. 1929	07 08	17 21	07 42	20 09	03 30	10 27	
19	Th	Duke of York b. 1960	07 06	17 22	08 52	21 18	04 23	11 18	
20	F	John Glenn orbits Earth 1962	07 04	17 24	10 29	22 55	05 05	12 20	
21	Sa	George Lansbury b. 1859	07 02	17 26	11 48	—	05 37	13 29	
22	Su	Florida ceded to US 1819	07 00	17 28	00 02	12 37	06 00	14 41	
23	M	Fascist Party founded 1919	06 58	17 30	00 47	13 15	06 19	15 55	
24	Tu	Shrove Tuesday	06 56	17 31	01 25	13 50	06 34	17 09	
25	W	Ash Wednesday	06 53	17 33	02 00	14 24	06 48	18 23	
26	Th	Fanny Cradock b. 1909	06 51	17 35	02 34	14 58	07 00	19 39	
27	F	Ellen Terry b. 1847	06 49	17 37	03 06	15 32	07 14	20 56	
28	Sa	Sir Stephen Spender b. 1909	06 47	17 39	03 37	16 04	07 28	22 16	

MOON'S PHASES FEBRUARY 2009

		Days	Hours	Mins
☽	First Quarter	2	23	13
○	Full Moon	9	14	49
☾	Last Quarter	16	21	37
●	New Moon	25	1	35

All times on this page are GMT

PREDICTIONS

The *Full Moon* on 9 February is an eclipse of the Moon and falls in Leo. In the UK there is likely to be a major reorganisation of the educational system, with recent reforms being abandoned and new procedures in place for university entrants, including new exams. Government plans to close further post offices will run into serious opposition and may be reversed. Great hope is signalled for the Middle East, and new peace talks may be announced. Israel and the Arabs will be discussing the allocation of water resources. Chinese pressure on Taiwan continues, possibly including military and naval manoeuvres.

The *New Moon* on 25 February falls in Pisces. Mercury, Mars and Jupiter are in a conjunction in Aquarius. The computer revolution is in full swing and we can expect an announcement about a new and even more revolutionary form of computer. There will be civil unrest in Iran, with a maximum chance of a change of government and opponents of the regime returning from exile. Volcanic activity along the Pacific Rim is likely around this time, as are new volcanic disturbances in Greenland. An ex-President of the US is likely to be receiving a singular honour from the UN.

A 6-y-o carrying 10st 5lb could prove victorious in the *Newbury Tote Gold Trophy* this month.

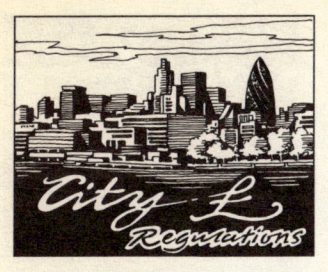

Predicted death of Yuri Andropov, 1984

MARCH

For High Water add 5h 30m for Bristol, 4h 23m for Hull, 0h 43m for Leith; subtract 2h 21m for Dublin, 1h 26m for Greenock, 2h 29m for Liverpool.

D of M	D of W	Festivals and Special Events for 2009	Sun at London Rises	Sun at London Sets	High Water at London Bridge am	High Water at London Bridge pm	Moon at London Rises	Moon at London Sets	Weather
			h m	h m	h m	h m	h m	h m	
1	Su	St David/first day in Lent	06 45	17 40	04 10	16 36	07 46	23 38	Northerly winds will bring about a sudden change to wintery weather early in the month. Frost and snowfall are likely everywhere except the south-west. By the close of the month it will be sunny.
2	M	Dame Naomi James b. 1949	06 43	17 42	04 42	17 11	08 09	—	
3	Tu	Lou Costello d. 1959	06 41	17 44	05 19	17 49	08 42	01 01	
4	W	Bernard Haitink b. 1929	06 38	17 46	06 02	18 37	09 27	02 19	
5	Th	Samantha Eggar b. 1939	06 36	17 47	07 03	19 48	10 30	03 25	
6	F	Aspirin patented 1899	06 34	17 49	08 31	21 19	11 47	04 15	
7	Sa	Telephone patent 1876	06 32	17 51	10 05	22 48	13 14	04 52	
8	Su	Kenneth Grahame b. 1859	06 29	17 52	11 33	—	14 42	05 18	
9	M	Commonwealth Day	06 27	17 54	00 02	12 37	16 09	05 38	
10	Tu	Bakerloo line opened 1906	06 25	17 56	01 00	13 29	17 33	05 54	
11	W	Sir Henry Tate b. 1819	06 23	17 58	01 46	14 14	18 55	06 08	
12	Th	St Gregory the Great	06 21	17 59	02 28	14 55	20 16	06 23	
13	F	Terence Brady b. 1939	06 18	18 01	03 06	15 32	21 35	06 38	
14	Sa	Albert Einstein b. 1879	06 16	18 03	03 41	16 05	22 53	06 56	
15	Su	Clothes rationing ended 1949	06 14	18 04	04 17	16 38	—	07 17	
16	M	Halabja massacre 1988	06 11	18 06	04 49	17 09	00 08	07 45	
17	Tu	St Patrick's Day	06 09	18 08	05 26	17 42	01 16	08 22	
18	W	Alex Higgins b. 1949	06 07	18 10	06 08	18 22	02 14	09 10	
19	Th	David Livingstone b. 1813	06 05	18 11	07 00	19 14	03 00	10 08	
20	F	Vernal equinox (11 44)	06 02	18 13	08 09	20 24	03 36	11 14	
21	Sa	Florenz Ziegfeld b. 1869	06 00	18 15	09 36	21 54	04 03	12 25	
22	Su	Mothering Sunday	05 58	18 16	11 07	23 23	04 23	13 37	
23	M	Roger Bannister b. 1929	05 55	18 18	—	12 01	04 40	14 51	
24	Tu	Tommy Trinder b. 1909	05 53	18 20	00 13	12 41	04 54	16 05	
25	W	Treaty of Rome signed 1957	05 51	18 21	00 53	13 18	05 08	17 21	
26	Th	Egypt-Israel treaty 1979	05 49	18 23	01 28	13 53	05 21	18 38	
27	F	Sir Henry Royce b. 1863	05 46	18 25	02 03	14 28	05 35	19 59	
28	Sa	Franco took Madrid 1939	05 44	18 26	02 37	15 02	05 52	21 22	
29	Su	Captain Scott d. 1912	05 42	18 28	03 11	15 37	06 14	22 47	
30	M	Queen Mother d. 2002	05 40	18 30	03 46	16 12	06 44	—	
31	Tu	Nikolai Gogol b. 1809	05 37	18 31	04 25	16 52	07 26	00 08	

MOON'S PHASES MARCH 2009

		Days	Hours	Mins
☽	First Quarter	4	7	6
○	Full Moon	11	2	38
☾	Last Quarter	18	17	47
●	New Moon	26	16	6

All times on this page are GMT (BST from 29 March + 1 hour)

PREDICTIONS

The *Full Moon* on 11 March falls in Virgo in an exact conjunction with Saturn and an opposition to Uranus. There is a risk that extremist groups will be employing newer and more dangerous tactics in order to achieve their objectives. In the UK there will be restructuring in the financial area, with tighter regulations for the Bank of England and City institutions. A major company is likely to collapse as a result of revelations regarding fraud. There are also indications of electoral reform but attempts to alter the House of Lords will be rebuffed. There is a high earthquake alert in Japan, Alaska and British Columbia.

The *New Moon* on 26 March falls in Aries in conjunction with Venus. Consumer spending picks up and there will be hopes of a high-street boom. Property prices will be in flux, with sharp rises in areas that are in demand but stagnation elsewhere. Major discoveries and development of new oil reserves should help keep the price of fuel stable. We can expect instability in Russia, with major anti-government demonstrations and vicious repression of protests. Towards the end of the month a famous newspaper group could announce that it intends to kill off a famous title.

The big national hunt venue, Cheltenham, is likely to see a young chaser (a 7-y-o) winning the *Gold Cup*.

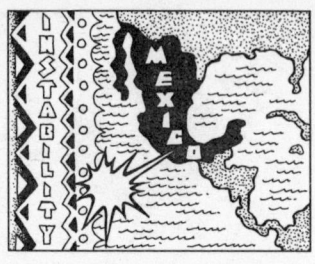

Predicted America close to depression, 2007

APRIL

For High Water add 5h 30m for Bristol, 4h 23m for Hull, 0h 43m for Leith; subtract 2h 21m for Dublin, 1h 26m for Greenock, 2h 29m for Liverpool.

D of M	D of W	Festivals and Special Events for 2009	Sun at London Rises	Sun at London Sets	High Water at London Bridge am	High Water at London Bridge pm	Moon at London Rises	Moon at London Sets	Weather
			h m	h m	h m	h m	h m	h m	
1	W	All Fools' Day	05 35	18 33	05 09	17 34	08 24	01 18	Winds will remain northerly up to mid-month, which will be an exceptionally cold period. Milder conditions can be expected for the last ten days, with a good deal of sunshine.
2	Th	Penelope Keith b. 1939	05 33	18 35	06 01	18 27	09 36	02 13	
3	F	Prince Ranier d. 2005	05 30	18 37	07 08	19 39	10 59	02 52	
4	Sa	NATO created 1949	05 28	18 38	08 30	21 02	12 25	03 21	
5	Su	Nigel Hawthorne b. 1929	05 26	18 40	09 54	22 28	13 50	03 42	
6	M	Richard I killed 1199	05 24	18 42	11 16	23 41	15 12	03 59	
7	Tu	Italy seized Albania 1939	05 22	18 43	—	12 18	16 33	04 14	
8	W	Sir Adrian Boult b. 1889	05 19	18 45	00 37	13 10	17 52	04 29	
9	Th	First day of Passover	05 17	18 47	01 25	13 52	19 11	04 43	
10	F	Good Friday	05 15	18 48	02 04	14 30	20 30	05 00	
11	Sa	William & Mary crowned 1689	05 13	18 50	02 41	15 05	21 46	05 20	
12	Su	Easter Day	05 11	18 52	03 16	15 36	22 58	05 46	
13	M	Easter Monday	05 08	18 53	03 50	16 05	—	06 19	
14	Tu	G.F. Handel d. 1759	05 06	18 55	04 22	16 34	00 01	07 03	
15	W	Hillsborough disaster 1989	05 04	18 57	04 59	17 06	00 53	07 57	
16	Th	Charlie Chaplin b. 1889	05 02	18 58	05 40	17 44	01 33	09 00	
17	F	James Last b. 1929	05 00	19 00	06 27	18 30	02 03	10 08	
18	Sa	Eire established 1949	04 58	19 02	07 28	19 31	02 26	11 20	
19	Su	Low Sunday	04 56	19 03	08 44	20 55	02 44	12 32	
20	M	Adolf Hitler b. 1889	04 53	19 05	10 03	22 19	02 59	13 45	
21	Tu	HM the Queen b. 1926	04 51	19 07	11 07	23 21	03 13	14 59	
22	W	Kathleen Ferrier b. 1912	04 49	19 08	11 56	—	03 26	16 15	
23	Th	St George's Day	04 47	19 10	00 09	12 40	03 40	17 34	
24	F	Sweets rationing ended 1949	04 45	19 12	00 50	13 19	03 57	18 58	
25	Sa	Oliver Cromwell b. 1559	04 43	19 13	01 29	13 57	04 17	20 24	
26	Su	Jill Dando murdered 1999	04 41	19 15	02 07	14 35	04 44	21 49	
27	M	Regent's Park opened 1828	04 39	19 17	02 47	15 15	05 23	23 05	
28	Tu	Mutiny on the *Bounty* 1789	04 37	19 18	03 30	15 56	06 16	—	
29	W	Duke Ellington b. 1899	04 35	19 20	04 17	16 41	07 26	00 07	
30	Th	Mary II b. 1662	04 34	19 22	05 07	17 30	08 47	00 52	

MOON'S PHASES APRIL 2009		Days	Hours	Mins
☽	First Quarter	2	14	34
○	Full Moon	9	14	56
☾	Last Quarter	17	13	36
●	New Moon	25	3	23

All times on this page are GMT (Add 1 hour BST)

PREDICTIONS

The *Full Moon* on 9 April falls in Libra and in a close aspect with Mars. There will be announcements of major new spending in the NHS and social services, but cuts in defence spending. However, there will be fresh demands on the British army, which may be in action in new areas, maybe Africa. West Africa is showing signs of instability and there is a high chance of a military coup or violent strife in Nigeria. There should be elections in Germany and these could result in either a change of government in Berlin or sweeping changes at state level. There will also be instability in Mexico, with possible violence in the south.

The *New Moon* on 25 April falls in Taurus, with Mars and Venus in an exact conjunction. The arts and entertainment industries will be flourishing, in spite of lower levels of government support. There may be a major legal case concerning satire or libels against senior government figures. We can expect pressure for a change of government in Afghanistan, which could affect Western interests adversely. International drug companies could be rapidly withdrawing a whole family of drugs that are suspected of contributing to psychological difficulties in people approaching puberty.

Favourites may well run best in Classic trials, whilst a 10-y-o carrying 10st could win at Aintree in the popular *Grand National*.

Predicted the General Strike to the day, 3 May 1926

MAY

For High Water add 5h 30m for Bristol, 4h 23m for Hull, 0h 43m for Leith; subtract 2h 21m for Dublin, 1h 26m for Greenock, 2h 29m for Liverpool.

D of M	D of W	Festivals and Special Events for 2009	Sun at London Rises	Sun at London Sets	High Water at London Bridge am	High Water at London Bridge pm	Moon at London Rises	Moon at London Sets	Weather
			h. m.	h. m.	h. m.	h. m.	h. m.	h. m.	
1	F	Gas industry nationalised 1949	04 32	19 23	06 05	18 27	10 13	01 24	Rather mixed weather throughout May, but the trend will be towards milder conditions. There will be above average rainfall, especially around mid-month. The last week will be fine and warm.
2	Sa	Jerome K. Jerome b. 1859	04 30	19 25	07 10	19 31	11 38	01 47	
3	Su	Eiffel Tower opened 1889	04 28	19 27	08 19	20 42	13 00	02 06	
4	M	Bank Holiday	04 26	19 28	09 33	22 00	14 20	02 21	
5	Tu	Maurice Maeterlinck d. 1949	04 24	19 30	10 49	23 13	15 38	02 35	
6	W	Channel Tunnel opened 1994	04 23	19 31	11 52	—	16 55	02 50	
7	Th	Robert Browning b. 1812	04 21	19 33	00 12	12 43	18 12	03 05	
8	F	VE Day 1945	04 19	19 35	01 00	13 26	19 29	03 24	
9	Sa	Wesek (Buddha Day)	04 18	19 36	01 41	14 04	20 42	03 47	
10	Su	Fred Astaire b. 1899	04 16	19 38	02 19	14 38	21 48	04 18	
11	M	Siam became Thailand 1949	04 14	19 39	02 54	15 09	22 45	04 57	
12	Tu	Berlin blockade ended 1949	04 13	19 41	03 27	15 37	23 29	05 48	
13	W	Zoe Wanamaker b. 1949	04 11	19 43	04 03	16 08	—	06 48	
14	Th	Cate Blanchett b. 1969	04 10	19 44	04 39	16 42	00 02	07 55	
15	F	James Mason b. 1909	04 08	19 46	05 19	17 19	00 28	09 05	
16	Sa	First Oscar ceremony 1929	04 07	19 47	06 02	18 01	00 47	10 16	
17	Su	Rogation Sunday	04 05	19 49	06 51	18 50	01 04	11 27	
18	M	Fred Perry b. 1909	04 04	19 50	07 49	19 52	01 18	12 39	
19	Tu	Simplon tunnel opened 1909	04 03	19 51	08 59	21 11	01 31	13 52	
20	W	Honoré de Balzac b. 1799	04 01	19 53	10 05	22 21	01 44	15 09	
21	Th	Ascension Day	04 00	19 54	11 06	23 20	01 59	16 29	
22	F	Arthur Conan Doyle b. 1859	03 59	19 56	11 58	—	02 18	17 54	
23	Sa	Bonnie and Clyde killed 1934	03 58	19 57	00 12	12 47	02 42	19 20	
24	Su	Dartmoor Prison opened 1809	03 56	19 58	01 00	13 32	03 15	20 43	
25	M	Spring Bank Holiday	03 55	20 00	01 46	14 16	04 03	21 54	
26	Tu	Sir Matt Busby b. 1909	03 54	20 01	02 33	15 01	05 08	22 47	
27	W	Habeas Corpus Act 1679	03 53	20 02	03 22	15 47	06 28	23 24	
28	Th	Armenia independent 1919	03 52	20 03	04 12	16 35	07 56	23 51	
29	F	Feast of Weeks	03 51	20 05	05 06	17 26	09 24	—	
30	Sa	Benny Goodman b. 1909	03 50	20 06	06 01	18 18	10 48	00 11	
31	Su	Whit Sunday/Pentecost	03 49	20 07	06 57	19 14	12 09	00 28	

MOON'S PHASES MAY 2009		Days	Hours	Mins
	First Quarter	1	20	44
	Full Moon	9	4	1
	Last Quarter	17	7	26
	New Moon	24	12	11
	First Quarter	31	3	22

All times on this page are GMT (Add 1 hour BST)

PREDICTIONS

The *Full Moon* on the 9th falls in Scorpio in the seventh house at London. Jupiter and Neptune are in a conjunction in the eleventh house at London. Public anger will be forthcoming as a result of fraud, waste and incompetence at Westminster. Cuba will continue its transition to a post-Castro phase and we can expect the first partially free elections ever, even though limits may exist. There will also be elections and government changes in South Africa; the ruling party will lose seats. Egypt is entering a revolutionary phase that will last two years, but there will be intensified government repression. There will also be instability across East Africa, with threats to the government of Tanzania. The Israeli government will be closing illegal settlements, prompting confrontation between settlers and the army.

The *New Moon* on the 24th falls in Gemini on the Midheaven at London. There will be major additions to the education budget in Britain; news of higher spending will arouse speculation regarding an Autumn election. There may be further pressure in Russia, which will now be at the point of choosing between western style democracy or benevolent dictatorship. New rules regarding the dumping of waste at sea will be suggested in the UN.

At Newmarket races, the *2,000 Guineas* is likely to be won by the favourite, whilst the *1,000 Guineas* may go to a joint second favourite.

Predicted Robert Maxwell fraud, 1991

JUNE

For High Water add 5h 30m for Bristol, 4h 23m for Hull, 0h 43m for Leith; subtract 2h 21m for Dublin, 1h 26m for Greenock, 2h 29m for Liverpool.

D of M	D of W	Festivals and Special Events for 2009	Sun at London Rises	Sun at London Sets	High Water at London Bridge am	High Water at London Bridge pm	Moon at London Rises	Moon at London Sets	Weather
			h m	h m	h m	h m	h m	h m	
1	M	*Thetis* submarine sank 1939	03 49	20 08	07 57	20 14	13 28	00 42	Thunderstorms will break the settled spell before mid-month, and thereafter westerly winds will bring frequent showers. Temperatures will soar to give some hot days by the end of the first week.
2	Tu	Coronation Day (1953)	03 48	20 09	09 04	21 25	14 44	00 57	
3	W	Ayatollah Khomeini d. 1989	03 47	20 10	10 14	22 38	16 01	01 12	
4	Th	Tiananmen Sq. massacre 1989	03 47	20 11	11 20	23 42	17 16	01 29	
5	F	Margaret Drabble b. 1939	03 46	20 12	—	12 15	18 30	01 51	
6	Sa	Diego Velasquez b. 1599	03 45	20 13	00 34	13 01	19 38	02 19	
7	Su	Trinity Sunday	03 45	20 14	01 19	13 41	20 38	02 55	
8	M	Sir Norman Hartnell d. 1979	03 44	20 15	02 00	14 16	21 26	03 42	
9	Tu	Gatwick Airport opened 1958	03 44	20 15	02 37	14 48	22 03	04 39	
10	W	Duke of Edinburgh b. 1921	03 44	20 16	03 13	15 20	22 31	05 44	
11	Th	Corpus Christi	03 43	20 17	03 49	15 53	22 52	06 53	
12	F	Baseball invented 1839	03 43	20 18	04 25	16 28	23 09	08 03	
13	Sa	Queen's official birthday	03 43	20 18	05 02	17 03	23 23	09 14	
14	Su	Steffi Graf. b. 1969	03 43	20 19	05 40	17 40	23 37	10 24	
15	M	Magna Carta 1215	03 42	20 19	06 20	18 19	23 49	11 35	
16	Tu	Enoch Powell b. 1912	03 42	20 20	07 04	19 04	—	12 48	
17	W	Edward I b. 1239	03 42	20 20	08 00	20 04	00 03	14 05	
18	Th	Eva Bartok b. 1929	03 42	20 20	09 08	21 22	00 20	15 25	
19	F	James I b. 1566	03 43	20 21	10 17	22 34	00 40	16 50	
20	Sa	Errol Flynn b. 1909	03 43	20 21	11 20	23 38	01 08	18 14	
21	Su	Summer solstice (05 46)	03 43	20 21	—	12 19	01 48	19 31	
22	M	Judy Garland d. 1969	03 43	20 21	00 37	13 12	02 45	20 34	
23	Tu	Battle of Plassey 1757	03 43	20 22	01 34	14 03	04 00	21 19	
24	W	Henry VIII crowned 1509	03 44	20 22	02 26	14 51	05 27	21 51	
25	Th	Custer's last stand 1876	03 44	20 22	03 16	15 39	05 69	22 15	
26	F	V&A Museum opened 1909	03 45	20 22	04 07	16 25	08 28	22 33	
27	Sa	Veterans' Day	03 45	20 21	04 56	17 11	09 53	22 49	
28	Su	Treaty of Versailles 1919	03 46	20 21	05 45	17 59	11 14	23 03	
29	M	St Peter	03 46	20 21	06 34	18 47	12 33	23 19	
30	Tu	Susan Hayward b. 1919	03 47	20 21	07 26	19 41	13 50	23 35	

MOON'S PHASES JUNE 2009

		Days	Hours	Mins
○	Full Moon	7	18	12
☾	Last Quarter	15	22	15
●	New Moon	22	19	35
☽	First Quarter	29	11	28

All times on this page are GMT (Add 1 hour BST)

PREDICTIONS

The *Full Moon* on the 7th falls in Sagittarius in the first house at London. This will bring about a powerful indication of confusion and muddle. Governments will say one thing but mean another, and policy statements will fall apart as soon as they are issued. In the UK, the government's popularity will slump. However, the business sector will be prospering. Property prices should show signs of recovery, and there may be talk of a new boom. Traditional areas make solid investments. Internet and computer technology will be risky and speculators must be prepared for losses as well as profits.

The *New Moon* on the 22nd falls in Cancer in an exact opposition with Pluto in Capricorn. Venus and Mars are in an exact conjunction. There will be a rise in global tension, but actual conflict is unlikely. Investment in the agricultural sector is favoured, especially in organics; and areas that depend on traditional technologies. There could be plans for new coal mines in the UK. Further changes are likely in Russia, and talks of a new President imply extreme instability. Libya is also facing major transformation, and there will be speculation that Colonel Gaddafi's long rule may be under threat.

When the *Derby* at Epsom gets underway early in the month, the result could well fall to the second favourite; likewise at the *Oaks* around the same time.

42

Predicted scandal in the White House, 1997

JULY

For High Water add 5h 30m for Bristol, 4h 23m for Hull, 0h 43m for Leith; subtract 2h 21m for Dublin, 1h 26m for Greenock, 2h 29m for Liverpool.

D of M	D of W	Festivals and Special Events for 2009	Sun at London Rises	Sun at London Sets	High Water at London Bridge am	High Water at London Bridge pm	Moon at London Rises	Moon at London Sets	Weather
1	W	Princess Diana b. 1961	03 47	20 21	08 24	20 42	15 06	23 55	Prepare for a wet first half of the month, with thunderstorms and possibly freak weather. The last two weeks will become more settled, with plenty of sunshine and a heatwave in the last few days.
2	Th	Thomas Cranmer b. 1489	03 48	20 20	09 29	21 56	16 21	—	
3	F	Brian Jones drowned 1969	03 49	20 20	10 39	23 10	17 30	00 21	
4	Sa	US Independence Day	03 50	20 19	11 44	—	18 33	00 54	
5	Su	Tom Mboya assassinated 1969	03 50	20 19	00 12	12 36	19 24	01 37	
6	M	Henry II d. 1189	03 51	20 18	01 03	13 19	20 04	02 31	
7	Tu	7/7 terrorist acts 2005	03 52	20 18	01 45	13 57	20 35	03 34	
8	W	Battle of Poltava 1709	03 53	20 17	02 23	14 33	20 58	04 42	
9	Th	Elias Howe b. 1819	03 54	20 16	02 58	15 06	21 16	05 53	
10	F	John Calvin b. 1509	03 55	20 15	03 33	15 40	21 31	07 04	
11	Sa	Lord Olivier d. 1989	03 56	20 15	04 07	16 12	21 44	08 14	
12	Su	Josiah Wedgwood b. 1730	03 57	20 14	04 41	16 45	21 57	09 24	
13	M	Bank Holiday in N. Ireland	03 58	20 13	05 14	17 16	22 10	10 35	
14	Tu	Grock the clown d. 1959	03 59	20 12	05 49	17 48	22 25	11 48	
15	W	St Swithin's Day	04 01	20 11	06 26	18 27	22 42	13 05	
16	Th	*Apollo 11* launch 1969	04 02	20 10	07 12	19 17	23 06	14 25	
17	F	Billie Holiday d. 1959	04 03	20 09	08 14	20 30	23 38	15 48	
18	Sa	Ballot Act 1872	04 04	20 08	09 32	21 56	—	17 07	
19	Su	Somoza resigned 1979	04 06	20 06	10 48	23 13	00 25	18 16	
20	M	Sir John Reith b. 1889	04 07	20 05	11 58	—	01 30	19 09	
21	Tu	First moon landing 1969	04 08	20 04	00 26	13 00	02 52	19 48	
22	W	Terence Stamp b. 1939	04 09	20 03	01 25	13 52	04 23	20 15	
23	Th	Michael Wilding b. 1912	04 11	20 01	02 19	14 40	05 56	20 36	
24	F	St Christina	04 12	20 00	03 06	15 25	07 26	20 54	
25	Sa	Blériot flew the Channel 1909	04 14	19 59	03 53	16 08	08 52	21 09	
26	Su	James Lovelock b. 1919	04 15	19 57	04 38	16 50	10 14	21 24	
27	M	B. of Killiecrankie 1689	04 16	19 56	05 21	17 33	11 34	21 41	
28	Tu	Post codes introduced 1959	04 18	19 54	06 04	18 15	12 53	22 00	
29	W	Benito Mussolini b. 1883	04 19	19 53	06 49	19 01	14 09	22 24	
30	Th	Peter Bogdanovich b. 1939	04 21	19 51	07 38	19 59	15 21	22 55	
31	F	Weimar Republic estab. 1919	04 22	19 49	08 35	21 09	16 26	23 35	

MOON'S PHASES JULY 2009

		Days	Hours	Mins
○	Full Moon	7	9	21
☾	Last Quarter	15	9	53
●	New Moon	22	2	35
☽	First Quarter	28	22	0

All times on this page are GMT (Add 1 hour BST)

PREDICTIONS

The *Full Moon* on the 7th is an eclipse in Capricorn. Jupiter and Neptune are in an exact conjunction and a square to Mars. This is a very warlike alignment, with conflicts taking place over both control of land and ideological fanaticism. The risks of more conflict between Israel and Palestine are at a peak but a radical peace agreement may be on the table. China may continue to make military threats against Taiwan, though may back down due to worries about its economy. Fringe religious cults cause problems for the authorities in America. In Britain we can expect extremes in weather between north and south.

The *New Moon* on the 22nd falls in Cancer in the second house at London. There will be scandals arising from incompetence and corruption afflicting the army and the Ministry of Defence. Major announcements can be expected regarding government spending, though allegations of massive waste are also likely. There will also be concern over the extent of the 'surveillance culture' and the collection of data on private individuals. Adverse weather conditions in Kashmir could lead to significant loss of life and new facts will be forthcoming about the true implications of ice loss at the Poles.

This month, a 4-y-o carrying just over 9st is most likely to win at Glorious Goodwood in the *Stewards' Cup* handicap.

43

Predicted atom bomb on Hiroshima, August 1945

AUGUST

For High Water add 5h 30m for Bristol, 4h 23m for Hull, 0h 43m for Leith; subtract 2h 21m for Dublin, 1h 26m for Greenock, 2h 29m for Liverpool.

D of M	D of W	Festivals and Special Events for 2009	Sun at London Rises	Sun at London Sets	High Water at London Bridge am	High Water at London Bridge pm	Moon at London Rises	Moon at London Sets	Weather
1	Sa	Britain abolished slavery 1834	04 24	19 48	09 46	22 38	17 21	—	An exceptionally warm month, though the sunshine will be broken by thunderstorms from time to time (especially in the south and east). The last week will see somewhat cooler weather.
2	Su	J.E. Montgolfier d. 1799	04 25	19 46	11 11	23 52	18 05	00 25	
3	M	Scottish Bank Holiday	04 27	19 44	—	12 13	18 38	01 25	
4	Tu	Britain declared war 1914	04 28	19 43	00 44	13 00	19 03	02 32	
5	W	Thomas Newcomen d. 1729	04 30	19 41	01 26	13 38	19 23	03 42	
6	Th	Alfred Lord Tennyson b. 1809	04 31	19 39	02 03	14 13	19 39	04 53	
7	F	Bernard Levin d. 2004	04 33	19 37	02 37	14 47	19 53	06 04	
8	Sa	F.W. Woolworth d. 1919	04 34	19 36	03 11	15 18	20 06	07 14	
9	Su	R. Leoncavallo d. 1919	04 36	19 34	03 43	15 49	20 18	08 25	
10	M	RAC founded 1897	04 38	19 32	04 14	16 19	20 32	09 37	
11	Tu	Pervez Musharraf b. 1943	04 39	19 30	04 46	16 49	20 49	10 52	
12	W	Ian Fleming d. 1964	04 41	19 28	05 19	17 21	21 09	12 09	
13	Th	Alfred Hitchcock b. 1899	04 42	19 26	05 52	17 58	21 37	13 29	
14	F	Troops deployed in NI 1969	04 44	19 24	06 34	18 46	22 16	14 48	
15	Sa	Princess Royal b. 1950	04 45	19 22	07 32	19 59	23 11	16 00	
16	Su	Margaret Mitchell d. 1949	04 47	19 20	08 55	21 32	—	16 58	
17	M	Rudolf Hess d. 1987	04 49	19 18	10 22	23 00	00 23	17 42	
18	Tu	Mini Minor unveiled 1959	04 50	19 16	11 42	—	01 49	18 14	
19	W	Sergei Diaghilev d. 1929	04 52	19 14	00 16	12 46	03 20	18 38	
20	Th	George Adamson murder 1989	04 53	19 12	01 15	13 38	04 51	18 57	
21	F	Hawaii became US state 1959	04 55	19 10	02 06	14 23	06 20	19 14	
22	Sa	First day of Ramadan	04 56	19 08	02 51	15 05	07 46	19 29	
23	Su	Geoff Capes b. 1949	04 58	19 06	03 33	15 46	09 09	19 46	
24	M	Emergency Powers bill 1939	05 00	19 03	04 12	16 25	10 31	20 04	
25	Tu	Anglo-Polish Treaty 1939	05 01	19 01	04 52	17 03	11 50	20 27	
26	W	Prince Albert b. 1819	05 03	18 59	05 30	17 41	13 06	20 55	
27	Th	Mountbatten murdered 1979	05 04	18 57	06 06	18 25	14 15	21 32	
28	F	J.W. Goethe b. 1749	05 06	18 55	06 50	19 19	15 15	22 19	
29	Sa	New Orleans disaster 2005	05 08	18 53	07 45	20 28	16 03	23 16	
30	Su	Children first evacuated 1939	05 09	18 50	08 54	22 00	16 40	—	
31	M	Bank Holiday (except Scotland)	05 11	18 48	10 31	23 28	17 07	00 21	

PREDICTIONS

The *Full Moon* on the 6th is an eclipse in Aquarius in the eighth house at London. Pluto is opposed the ascendant at London. France is in a buoyant state and government popularity is based on compromise with traditional forces, such as the unions. We should look out for problems in the German economy, with a major German carmaker needing financial assistance. Japan is entering an expansionary period and far-sighted investors will find bargains in the Japanese markets. New sources of power are under discussion and there are likely to be talks in the UN about limiting the amount of land given over to growing crops for bio-fuel worldwide.

The *New Moon* on the 20th falls in Leo. In the UK we can expect royal celebrations, such as an engagement or marriage. Iraq will enter a new phase, bringing a turning point leading to peace. India is also in a state of flux, and a new, strong leader could emerge. The country may also expect major flooding. The Philippines, Indonesia and western Australia may also experience extreme weather, with flash floods likely and calls for assistance stretching emergency centres worldwide. Russia is likely to make threats against some of its neighbours and may turn off gas and oil supplies.

At the York *Ebor Handicap*, the winning horse is most likely to be a 4-y-o carrying around 8st 7lb.

MOON'S PHASES AUGUST 2009		Days	Hours	Mins
○ Full Moon		6	0	5
☾ Last Quarter		13	18	55
● New Moon		20	10	2
☽ First Quarter		27	11	42

All times on this page are GMT (Add 1 hour BST)

Predicted a hike in oil prices, 2008

SEPTEMBER

For High Water add 5h 30m for Bristol, 4h 23m for Hull, 0h 43m for Leith; subtract 2h 21m for Dublin, 1h 26m for Greenock, 2h 29m for Liverpool.

D of M	D of W	Festivals and Special Events for 2009	Sun at London Rises	Sun at London Sets	High Water at London Bridge am	High Water at London Bridge pm	Moon at London Rises	Moon at London Sets	Weather
1	Tu	Hitler invaded Poland 1939	05 12	18 46	11 47	—	17 29	01 30	An unsettled start to the month, cool everywhere and heavy rain at times. A gradual increase in warm sunshine can be expected from the second week, giving rise to a long spell of Indian summer.
2	W	Battle of Actium 31 BC	05 14	18 44	00 20	12 34	17 46	02 41	
3	Th	War declared on Germany 1939	05 16	18 41	01 01	13 12	18 01	03 52	
4	F	Georges Simenon d. 1989	05 17	18 39	01 36	13 46	18 14	05 03	
5	Sa	ITV in colour 1969	05 19	18 37	02 09	14 19	18 27	06 14	
6	Su	Kay Kendall d. 1959	05 20	18 35	02 41	14 49	18 41	07 27	
7	M	Elia Kazan b. 1909	05 22	18 32	03 12	15 20	18 57	08 41	
8	Tu	Richard Strauss d. 1949	05 23	18 30	03 44	15 50	19 16	09 58	
9	W	John Curry, skater, b. 1949	05 25	18 28	04 17	16 22	19 41	11 17	
10	Th	Arnold Palmer b. 1929	05 27	18 26	04 49	16 59	20 16	12 35	
11	F	Battle of Malplaquet 1709	05 28	18 23	05 26	17 40	21 04	13 48	
12	Sa	Haile Selassie deposed 1974	05 30	18 21	06 08	18 32	22 08	14 50	
13	Su	S. Bandaranaike d. 1959	05 31	18 19	07 08	19 50	23 26	15 38	
14	M	Lunik II moon landing 1959	05 33	18 16	08 34	21 23	—	16 13	
15	Tu	Prince Harry b. 1984	05 35	18 14	10 05	22 52	00 52	16 39	
16	W	Sir Alexander Korda b. 1893	05 36	18 12	11 27	—	02 21	17 00	
17	Th	Ethel M. Dell d. 1939	05 38	18 09	00 04	12 29	03 49	17 17	
18	F	Samuel Johnson b. 1709	05 39	18 07	01 00	13 18	05 15	17 34	
19	Sa	Jewish New Year (5770)	05 41	18 05	01 48	14 03	06 39	17 50	
20	Su	Battle of Alma 1854	05 43	18 02	02 30	14 42	08 03	18 08	
21	M	St Matthew	05 44	18 00	03 09	15 20	09 25	18 29	
22	Tu	Autumn equinox (21 19)	05 46	17 58	03 46	15 57	10 44	18 55	
23	W	Sigmund Freud d. 1939	05 47	17 56	04 21	16 34	11 58	19 29	
24	Th	F. Scott Fitzgerald b. 1896	05 49	17 53	04 55	17 11	13 03	20 13	
25	F	Ronnie Barker b. 1929	05 51	17 51	05 27	17 52	13 56	21 07	
26	Sa	S. Bandaranaike d. 1959	05 52	17 49	06 06	18 44	14 37	22 09	
27	Su	Dame Gracie Fields d. 1979	05 54	17 46	06 57	19 50	15 09	23 17	
28	M	Day of Atonement	05 56	17 44	08 07	21 13	15 32	—	
29	Tu	Sir Billy Butlin b. 1899	05 57	17 42	09 36	22 46	15 51	00 27	
30	W	Identity cards issued 1939	05 59	17 40	11 06	23 45	16 07	01 38	

MOON'S PHASES SEPTEMBER 2009

		Days	Hours	Mins
○	Full Moon	4	16	3
☾	Last Quarter	12	2	16
●	New Moon	18	18	44
☽	First Quarter	26	4	50

All times on this page are GMT (Add 1 hour BST)

PREDICTIONS

The *Full Moon* on the 4th falls in Pisces in the second house at London. Financial instability returns in the UK, and there will be announcements of emergency reforms in the tax and pension systems, including cuts in pensions for civil servants. The Royal Family could be experiencing difficulties, with tabloid allegations against a minor member. Turkey is entering a period of instability, but fears of a take-over by Islamic fundamentalists are unfounded. Pakistan could be in a state of chaos, and it is unlikely that the government can control the country. The far west of Africa, the Atlantic coast of Europe, and the Midwest of the USA may be subject to violent weather conditions.

The *New Moon* on the 18th falls in Virgo in a close conjunction with Mercury and Saturn. There will be serious announcements concerning transport and strikes or disruption on the roads and railways. Local government workers may strike throughout the month. There will be changes in the exam system in British schools and the A Level may now be considered a second-rate qualification. We can expect popular protest and elections in Egypt. China will be heading for major reforms as the Communist Party relaxes its grip on government.

The oldest classic, the *St Leger* at Doncaster, may go to a well-backed filly. Meanwhile at Ayr, the *Gold Cup* could see a 4-y-o sprinter as the winning horse.

Predicted American finance close to melt-down, 2008

OCTOBER

For High Water add 5h 30m for Bristol, 4h 23m for Hull, 0h 43m for Leith; subtract 2h 21m for Dublin, 1h 26m for Greenock, 2h 29m for Liverpool.

D of M	D of W	Festivals and Special Events for 2009	Sun at London Rises	Sun at London Sets	High Water at London Bridge am	High Water at London Bridge pm	Moon at London Rises	Moon at London Sets	Weather
1	Th	St Pancras station op. 1869	06 00	17 37	11 58	—	16 21	02 48	
2	F	Mahatma Gandhi b. 1869	06 02	17 35	00 27	12 39	16 35	04 00	
3	Sa	First day of Tabernacles	06 04	17 33	01 03	13 12	16 48	05 12	
4	Su	Rembrandt d. 1669	06 05	17 31	01 36	13 45	17 04	06 26	
5	M	Paddington train crash 1999	06 07	17 28	02 09	14 17	17 23	07 43	
6	Tu	Moulin Rouge opened 1889	06 09	17 26	02 42	14 51	17 46	09 03	Despite a stormy start in the north and west, this will be a generally mild month with a good deal of sunshine everywhere. Rain will be confined to the last week and night frosts are unlikely to occur.
7	W	Mario Lanza d. 1959	06 10	17 24	03 15	15 26	18 19	10 23	
8	Th	Baroness Boothroyd b. 1929	06 12	17 22	03 50	16 03	19 03	11 38	
9	F	Paul Hunter d. 2006	06 14	17 19	04 28	16 45	20 02	12 44	
10	Sa	Battle of Tours 732	06 15	17 17	05 09	17 33	21 15	13 35	
11	Su	Boer War began 1899	06 17	17 15	05 56	18 33	22 37	14 13	
12	M	Robert Stephenson d. 1859	06 19	17 13	07 01	19 50	—	14 42	
13	Tu	Coronation of Henry IV 1399	06 20	17 11	08 23	21 13	00 02	15 04	
14	W	*Royal Oak* sunk 1939	06 22	17 09	09 47	22 36	01 27	15 22	
15	Th	Walter Sisulu freed 1989	06 24	17 06	11 04	23 44	02 51	15 38	
16	F	Lee Harvey Oswald b. 1939	06 26	17 04	—	12 06	04 14	15 54	
17	Sa	Frédéric Chopin d. 1849	06 27	17 02	00 39	12 57	05 36	16 11	
18	Su	San Francisco earthquake 1989	06 29	17 00	01 25	13 41	06 58	16 31	
19	M	Alfred Dreyfus b. 1859	06 31	16 58	02 06	14 20	08 19	16 55	
20	Tu	Anthony Quayle d. 1989	06 33	16 56	02 44	14 56	09 36	17 26	
21	W	Trafalgar Day (1805)	06 34	16 54	03 19	15 33	10 46	18 06	
22	Th	Doris Lessing b. 1919	06 36	16 52	03 51	16 10	11 45	18 57	
23	F	Zane Grey b. 1939	06 38	16 50	04 22	16 48	12 32	19 57	
24	Sa	Treaty of Westphalia 1648	06 40	16 48	04 55	17 27	13 07	21 03	
25	Su	Battle of Balaklava 1854	06 41	16 46	05 31	18 15	13 34	22 12	
26	M	London buses red 1929	06 43	16 44	06 16	19 12	13 54	23 22	
27	Tu	John Cleese b. 1939	06 45	16 42	07 18	20 24	14 11	—	
28	W	Francis Bacon b. 1909	06 47	16 40	08 41	21 41	14 26	00 32	
29	Th	Wall Street crash 1929	06 48	16 38	10 03	22 49	14 40	01 42	
30	F	Sir Barnes Wallis d. 1979	06 50	16 36	11 06	23 40	14 54	02 53	
31	Sa	Hallowe'en	06 52	16 35	11 52	—	15 09	04 06	

MOON'S PHASES OCTOBER 2009

		Days	Hours	Mins
○	Full Moon	4	6	10
☾	Last Quarter	11	8	56
●	New Moon	18	5	33
☽	First Quarter	26	0	42

All times on this page are GMT (BST to October 25 + 1 hour).

PREDICTIONS

The *Full Moon* on the 4th falls in Aries on the seventh cusp at London. There will be failures in communication, technological breakdown and dangerous hacking into government and financial computer systems. We can expect widespread dissatisfaction with politics and the government may lose a major vote in Parliament. However, the Conservative Party is still liable to bouts of confusion and is not yet sufficiently trusted as a party of government. The EU will be restructuring, with further powers moving from national government to Brussels. London's airports may be in a state of gridlock with warnings about crowded airspace causing concern for travellers.

The *New Moon* on the 18th falls in Libra in close aspect with Saturn, Uranus and Neptune. This is, in general, a suitable moment for the launch of new enterprises. In the UK there will be major new entertainments for children, a new blockbuster book or film and a surprising resurgence in the popularity of religion. There may be breakthroughs in medical science, especially in surgery, with the use of robots and microscopic machines to offer new solutions to chronic problems. New and radical cancer cures may also be in the news but optimism could be premature.

At Newmarket this month, the *Cesarewitch Handicap* may go to a 4-y-o outsider carrying 9st 1lb, whilst the *Cambridgeshire* may see a 3-y-o (weighted with 8st 6lb) win.

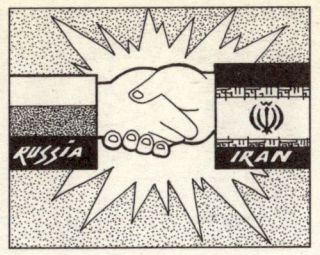

Predicted the abdication of Edward VIII, 1936

NOVEMBER

For High Water add 5h 30m for Bristol, 4h 23m for Hull, 0h 43m for Leith; subtract 2h 21m for Dublin, 1h 26m for Greenock, 2h 29m for Liverpool.

D of M	D of W	Festivals and Special Events for 2009	Sun at London Rises	Sun at London Sets	High Water at London Bridge am	High Water at London Bridge pm	Moon at London Rises	Moon at London Sets	Weather
1	Su	Pony Club founded 1929	06 54	16 33	00 22	12 33	15 26	05 22	Considerable amounts of fog can be expected in southern and eastern counties, particularly in the first fortnight. The next two weeks will be mild for the time of year, but rain is likely in most areaas.
2	M	M1 opened 1959	06 55	16 31	01 00	13 11	15 49	06 42	
3	Tu	Larry Holmes b. 1949	06 57	16 29	01 38	13 49	16 18	08 03	
4	W	Tutankhamun uncovered 2007	06 59	16 28	02 14	14 27	16 59	09 23	
5	Th	Guy Fawkes Night	07 01	16 26	02 52	15 08	17 55	10 34	
6	F	Nigel Havers b. 1949	07 03	16 24	03 33	15 53	19 05	11 31	
7	Sa	Su Pollard b. 1949	07 04	16 23	04 15	16 41	20 26	12 14	
8	Su	Remembrance Sunday	07 06	16 21	05 02	17 34	21 50	12 45	
9	M	Katherine Hepburn b. 1909	07 08	16 19	05 55	18 34	23 15	13 09	
10	Tu	UN condemn apartheid 1959	07 10	16 18	06 56	19 42	—	13 28	
11	W	Armistice signed 1918	07 11	16 16	08 06	20 55	00 37	13 44	
12	Th	Revd Chad Varah b. 1911	07 13	16 15	09 20	22 11	01 58	14 00	
13	F	St Augustine b. 354	07 15	16 14	10 36	23 19	03 18	14 16	
14	Sa	Prince of Wales b. 1948	07 17	16 12	11 40	—	04 38	14 35	
15	Su	Brazil a republic 1889	07 18	16 11	00 15	12 33	05 58	14 57	
16	M	Suez Canal opened 1869	07 20	16 09	01 03	13 18	07 16	15 25	
17	Tu	Emperor Vespasian b. 9	07 22	16 08	01 43	13 59	08 28	16 01	
18	W	Johnny Mercer b. 1909	07 24	16 07	02 21	14 38	09 32	16 47	
19	Th	Dennis Taylor b. 1949	07 25	16 06	02 55	15 15	10 24	17 44	
20	F	Battle of Quiberon 1759	07 27	16 05	03 27	15 51	11 04	18 48	
21	Sa	Quentin Crisp d. 1999	07 29	16 03	03 58	16 29	11 34	19 57	
22	Su	Cecil Sharp b. 1859	07 30	16 02	04 32	17 07	11 57	21 06	
23	M	Billy the Kid b. 1859	07 32	16 01	05 07	17 49	12 15	22 16	
24	Tu	BOAC formed 1939	07 33	16 00	05 48	18 37	12 31	23 25	
25	W	Charles Kennedy b. 1959	07 35	15 59	06 36	19 32	12 45	—	
26	Th	Tina Turner b. 1939	07 36	15 59	07 35	20 38	12 58	00 34	
27	F	Fanny Kemble b. 1809	07 38	15 58	08 51	21 43	13 12	01 45	
28	Sa	Lady Astor an MP 1919	07 39	15 57	10 00	22 43	13 28	02 58	
29	Su	First Sunday in Advent	07 41	15 56	10 59	23 37	13 48	04 16	
30	M	St Andrew's Day	07 42	15 56	11 51	—	14 14	05 36	

MOON'S PHASES NOVEMBER 2009

		Days	Hours	Mins
○	Full Moon	2	19	14
☾	Last Quarter	9	15	56
●	New Moon	16	19	14
☽	First Quarter	24	21	39

All times on this page are GMT

PREDICTIONS

The *Full Moon* on the 2nd falls in Taurus in the eleventh house at London and in a square to Mars. There is likely to be good news for the arts, with increased funding and international success for British performers. There will also be shocking revelations of child abuse and international child trafficking. New laws concerning children's rights will be passed later in the month. Internationally, Russia is under extreme pressure, and the chance of a substantial change of government is now at its peak. Such a move is bound to have major international consequences. There may also be policy changes in Iran. Of concern to the USA is the developing alliance between Russia and Iran, and tension between Iran and the Gulf States.

The *New Moon* on the 16th falls in Scorpio in the fifth house at London, a square to Neptune. Hopes for Middle East peace are high, as the US administration puts more pressure on both sides to reach agreement, though Israel continues to prevaricate. The Russian economy is almost certain to be booming and there may be discoveries of further reserves of oil in Siberia. The chances of earth tremors are high, with Iran, California and northern Mexico under most pressure.

The *November Handicap* meeting at Doncaster could bring a win from a 3-y-o carrying 8st 6lb.

47

2010 Old Moore's Almanack on sale June 2009

DECEMBER

For High Water add 5h 30m for Bristol, 4h 23m for Hull, 0h 43m for Leith; subtract 2h 21m for Dublin, 1h 26m for Greenock, 2h 29m for Liverpool.

D of M	D of W	Festivals and Special Events for 2009	Sun at London Rises	Sun at London Sets	High Water at London Bridge am	High Water at London Bridge pm	Moon at London Rises	Moon at London Sets	Weather
			h m	h m	h m	h m	h m	h m	
1	Tu	Lee Trevino b. 1939	07 44	15 55	00 25	12 40	14 50	06 58	
2	W	John Brown hanged 1859	07 45	15 54	01 11	13 26	15 41	08 14	
3	Th	P.A. Renoir d. 1919	07 47	15 54	01 55	14 13	16 47	09 20	
4	F	Jack Payne d. 1969	07 48	15 53	02 38	14 59	18 07	10 09	
5	Sa	Sir Henry Tate d. 1899	07 49	15 53	03 23	15 49	19 34	10 46	Early in the month strong northerly winds will bring some snowfall, and a period of wintry rain will follow. Although the Christmas period will turn quite mild, a cold snap will occur at the year's end.
6	Su	St Nicholas	07 50	15 52	04 10	16 38	21 01	11 12	
7	M	Pearl Harbor 1941	07 52	15 52	04 57	17 30	22 26	11 33	
8	Tu	James Galway b. 1939	07 53	15 52	05 47	18 25	23 48	11 51	
9	W	John Cassavetes b. 1929	07 54	15 52	06 40	19 24	—	12 07	
10	Th	Felice Orsini b. 1819	07 55	15 52	07 39	20 27	01 08	12 23	
11	F	Cliff Michelmore b. 1919	07 56	15 51	08 47	21 36	02 26	12 40	
12	Sa	Robert Browning d. 1889	07 57	15 51	10 00	22 46	03 45	13 00	
13	Su	B. of River Plate began 1939	07 58	15 51	11 10	23 47	05 02	13 26	
14	M	George Washington d. 1799	07 59	15 51	—	12 11	06 15	13 59	
15	Tu	Nylon production began 1939	08 00	15 52	00 39	13 01	07 22	14 41	
16	W	Napoleon's divorce 1809	08 01	15 52	01 24	13 45	08 17	15 34	
17	Th	*Graf Spee* scuttled 1939	08 01	15 52	02 03	14 24	09 01	16 36	
18	F	Islamic New Year	08 02	15 52	02 38	15 02	09 35	17 43	
19	Sa	Stella Gibbons d. 1989	08 03	15 53	03 11	15 39	10 00	18 53	
20	Su	Noriega overthrown 1989	08 03	15 53	03 43	16 14	10 20	20 02	
21	M	Winter solstice (17 47)	08 04	15 54	04 17	16 49	10 36	21 11	
22	Tu	Ceaucescu overthrown 1989	08 04	15 54	04 50	17 26	10 50	22 19	
23	W	Maurice Denham b. 1909	08 05	15 55	05 26	18 04	11 04	23 28	
24	Th	Christmas Eve	08 05	15 55	06 02	18 46	11 17	—	
25	F	Christmas Day	08 05	15 56	06 44	19 34	11 32	00 38	
26	Sa	Boxing Day/Tsunami 2004	08 06	15 57	07 36	20 37	11 49	01 52	
27	Su	Fanny Cradock d. 1994	08 06	15 57	08 49	21 46	12 11	03 08	
28	M	Holiday	08 06	15 58	10 05	22 52	12 41	04 28	
29	Tu	William Gladstone b. 1809	08 06	15 59	11 13	23 54	13 23	05 47	
30	W	Tracy Ullman b. 1959	08 06	16 00	—	12 15	14 22	06 59	
31	Th	New Year's Eve/Hogmanay	08 06	16 01	00 50	13 12	15 37	07 57	

MOON'S PHASES DECEMBER 2009		Days	Hours	Mins
○ Full Moon		2	7	30
☾ Last Quarter		9	0	13
● New Moon		16	12	2
☽ First Quarter		24	17	36
○ Full Moon		31	19	13

Calendarial data reproduced with permission from HM National Almanac Office © Particle Physics and Astronomy Research Council. Tidal predictions computed by the Proudman Oceanographic Laboratory © reserved.

PREDICTIONS

The *Full Moon* on the 2nd falls in Gemini on the seventh cusp at London. Mars is in opposition with Jupiter and Neptune. This favours religious crusaders from all backgrounds, and we will hear much talk of Jihad or of restoring Christian values. There may also be further substantial rises in the price of oil, which will benefit oil-producing nations including Saudi Arabia and Venezuela, but hit oil-importing nations, such as Japan. Grain reserves in the West could be at an all-time low.

The *Full Moon* on the 16th falls in Sagittarius in a conjunction with Venus and a square to Uranus, which is rising at the UK. There may be unexpected peace moves in the Muslim world, involving the Afghan war, with a possibility of joint Iranian-Pakistani initiatives. In the UK there may be spy scandals, prison breaks and scandals over the care of the mentally ill.

The *Full Moon* on the 31st is an eclipse in Cancer. In the UK, opinion polls show government popularity sliding and election fever begins. There will be disruption to the travel system, especially maritime communications. Ferry services are likely to be hit worldwide. There may also be major instances of piracy in the Pacific.

The *King George VI Chase*, at Kempton on Boxing Day, may go to an Irish-trained favourite.

OLD MOORE'S
LUCKY NUMBER TELEPHONE DRAW

£42,000 TO BE WON
★ CASH PRIZES EVERY MONTH ★

- **Your unique number is on the back cover of this Almanack.**
- **Ring 0906 470 9025 each month to hear if you have won.**
- **There is a star prize of £5,000 which will be carried forward to each month's draw until it is won and there are ten other cash prizes each month.**

Remember to ring 0906 470 9025
between the 1st and 25th of each month to hear the winning numbers

HOW TO CLAIM YOUR PRIZE:
If you have a winning number, telephone Foulsham on **01753 526769 by the 25th of the month of the draw,** giving your name, address and winning number – or you can write to the address shown below. You will be asked to prove your entitlement by sending in your Almanack, or the allocated number page, by the month's end, by registered post. Once we are satisfied that the claim is *bona fide*, we will then return it to you with your *winning cheque*.

Terms and conditions

1. No purchase is necessary. If a number does not appear on the back page of your Almanack or you want to enter by post, send a stamped addressed envelope to Foulsham at the address below and you will be sent a number.
2. Telephone calls on 0906 470 9025 cost 60p per minute at all times. (Mobiles and other network providers may charge higher rates.)
3. The Lucky Number draw will run from the 1st July 2008 to the 25th December 2009. The numbers, which will be selected at random, will be drawn on the first day of each month. The first number drawn will win £500, the next five numbers will each win £500 and the next five numbers drawn will each win £100. There will be two extra £500 prizes in December. If the £5,000 prize is not claimed by 28th July 2008 and validated, it will be carried forward each month, until the expiry of the draw, under a new number, until it is claimed.
4. The draw is open to all UK residents aged 18 and over, except employees of Foulsham, their printers and binders, ATS and Seymour.
5. Claims must reach Foulsham by the 28th day of the month of the draw, otherwise they will be void. Successful claims will only be paid out on receipt of the complete 2009 Almanack or allocated page number. Proof of posting will not be taken as proof of delivery.
6. Winning numbers will be returned to winners and will continue to be used for the remainder of the draws.
7. We reserve the right to involve winners in any publicity.
8. Numbers which appear to have been altered or tampered with will not be accepted.
9. A list of winning numbers can be obtained by sending a stamped addressed envelope to Foulsham at Bennetts Close, Cippenham, Slough, Berks SL1 5AP.
10. The editor's decision is final.

★ **YOUR INDIVIDUAL LUCKY NUMBER IS PRINTED ON THE BACK OF THIS ALMANACK** ★

VIRGO BORN PEOPLE
Birthdays: 24 August to 23 September inclusive
Planet: Mercury. Birthstone: Sardonyx. Lucky day: Wednesday

Keynote for the Year: *Look out for opportunities for improvement in the workplace. The extra responsibilities and effort will, eventually, be worth it.*

JANUARY: Main Trends: 3–5 You should find it easy to work with other people and will be rewarded if you put your energy into relating to and communicating with others. **19–20** Practical affairs are favourably highlighted – capitalise on your ability to engage support to bring success at work. **21–22** Make a little effort and you should be soaking up the spotlight and receiving an enthusiastic reaction. **Key Dates: Highs 14–15** Those in power should be receptive to your requests. This is a good time to get your own way! **Lows 28–30** Daily life may be an uphill struggle – take it easy.

FEBRUARY: Main Trends: 3–4 This is the time to be making changes in your life. **5–6** Be patient at work and don't take things for granted – work carefully and move slowly towards your goals. **18–19** Use your social drive and benefit from dealings with close friends or partners – not the time to stay in! **Key Dates: Highs 10–11** With a little faith and some clever manipulation you should be able to achieve what you've set your mind on. **Lows 25–26** You may be all at sea with certain relationships. Fulfil your obligations as calmer times are not far away!

MARCH: Main Trends: 10–11 Relationships – in business meetings, social life or personal encounters – can be fulfilling and worthwhile, so focus on this area. **15–16** Take care when trying to get your own way as this may not be the best time for negotiations. **24–25** Look to intimate relationships as they can bring fulfilment. Also make this a phase of positive transformation by clearing out any deadwood. **Key Dates: Highs 8–9** A favourable time to be pushing ahead while you have the motivation and luck on your side. **Lows 21–23** There may be major delay to a plan of action. Consider waiting until this low point is over.

APRIL: Main Trends: 12–13 Capitalise on your ability to make progress with practical issues and enjoy harmony at work – you should be able to make a good job of just about anything. **18–19** Check out whatever opportunities are available for expanding your interests and personal horizons – you need a change. **24–25** Focus on self-improvement and getting rid of anything that is not essential. Make the most of the help that is available. **Key Dates: Highs 6–7** A hopeful trend which may signify fresh changes – the rest is up to you, so be sure to take the initiative. **Lows 20–22** Keep a low profile and restore your energy as you are unlikely to make progress.

MAY: Main Trends: 13–14 Concentrate on widening your personal horizons and enjoy social encounters as these may help you to understand life better. **20–21** Capitalise on your leadership skills and ability to work well with those in authority at work. Constructive activity should help to further your ambitions. **30–31** You may prove highly competitive – even pushy – when it comes to discussing things with others; beware of sounding like a know-all! **Key Dates: Highs 3–4; 30–31** Make the most of your winning ways and an element of luck in major ventures to stay one step ahead. **Lows 18–19** Try to focus your ideas. If this fails, rest and recuperate.

JUNE: Main Trends: 6–8 Focus on personal freedom, especially when it comes to travel plans – the further you go, the better. **16–17** Take advantage of this positive highlight on career issues and don't ignore the importance of helpful input from others to your future plans. **21–22** Ensure that this is a fulfilling period socially and look for success as a result of teamwork. **Key Dates: Highs 1; 27–28** Put

Virgo: plan into your lucky times

your increased physical energy and initiative to excellent use! **Lows 14–15** Everyday life may be disappointing and there may be missed opportunities – don't expect to make progress.

JULY: Main Trends: 3–5 Capitalise on your charm to relate well to the crowd. **6–7** Prepare for issues coming to a head career-wise. Concentrate on new ideas and change – don't be afraid of being a go-getter. **22–23** Keep a low profile during this phase as your feelings may not be in sync with others and this may result in a clash. **Key Dates: Highs 24–25** This is the time to be bold when going after what you want. Make the most of your boundless optimism. **Lows 11–13** Life may be thrown into disarray. Are you up to the challenge?

AUGUST: Main Trends: 1–2 Be prepared for a lively period of social activity. Look to new contacts acting as a catalyst for certain ideas and interests. **23–24** Make the most of this personal boost and look out for material opportunities. This is a good time to be independent in your activities. **26–27** A negative influence for personal relationships – you may find it hard to say no to others, but don't be a doormat. **Key Dates: Highs 21–22** The time is right to pursue personal dreams and schemes while good fortune is on your side. **Lows 7–9** Take a careful approach to goals and ambitions and suspend major decisions.

SEPTEMBER Main Trends: 19–20 Make a little effort and communications should flow smoothly. Be prepared for news that should excite you into action! **21–22** Capitalise on the good impression you can make on others – the spotlight is on you, and you may well enjoy a little drama in your life. **23–25** Concentrate on pursuing growth in financial developments. There should be scope for building upon recent starts or getting a new practical project under way. **Key Dates: Highs 17–18** Make an early start with plans while you have the ability to move ahead and have superior judgement. **Lows 4–5** Expect personal pressures to contend with and a lack of patience – suspend whatever is truly important.

OCTOBER: Main Trends: 10–12 Look to practical ideas for opportunities for improvement and focus on getting the most from finance. **16–17** Take advantage of the scope for attracting life's little luxuries: a piece of minor luck could make finances even more secure. **23–24** You may find yourself at the forefront of vital communication issues. Attend to a variety of tasks in order to attract success. **Key Dates: Highs 14–15** Have faith in yourself and your larger than life personality should make a powerful impression on others. **Lows 1; 28–30** Life may put obstacles in your way that require a rethink on your part – take a more wary approach to life.

NOVEMBER: Main Trends: 8–10 A positive mental outlook makes this an excellent time for learning and communicating. Look to meetings with others to inspire brand new ideas. **16–17** Make the most of this rewarding time on the domestic front – partners may conspire to make things lively! **22–24** Once more, you should derive pleasure from your domestic life. Focus on family get-togethers and reliving the good old days. **Key Dates: Highs 11–12** Make the effort to exploit certain possibilities. You can get so much more out of life, so think big and expect the best. **Lows 25–26** Avoid the competitive world and don't make any hasty decisions while your powers of judgement are limited.

DECEMBER: Main Trends: 1–2 Take a back seat when it comes to your ambitions – be willing to put others first and put off certain professional issues. **20–21** Capitalise on your charm to get the best from other people. This is a good period for romantic pursuits so be on the lookout for new admirers. **26–27** The planetary focus is on romance and the world of fun and pleasure. Put your commanding personality to good use and assume the starring role. **Key Dates: Highs 8–9** Make the most of your high energy levels and positive thinking. This is a great time for new beginnings and looking for help. **Lows 22–23** Energy levels may be low and decisions may go awry – don't expect too much of yourself.

LIBRA BORN PEOPLE
Birthdays: 24 September to 23 October inclusive
Planet: Venus. Birthstone: Opal. Lucky day: Friday

Keynote for the Year: *There may be high points in love and romance, so look ahead to new opportunities. Be prepared to deal with an issue from the past once and for all.*

JANUARY: Main Trends: 6–7 A largely secure period when you can make steady progress; make the most of this by seeking employment or promotion and developing new skills. **19–20** This could be a promising time for social developments, so seek out social stimulation and a variety of tasks to perform. You will not thrive on your own. **21–23** Your home life may be busy and active, but also interesting and uplifting. This is the time to get in touch with your roots. **Key Dates: Highs 16–17** Look out for the right kinds of chances when it comes to achieving your aims, and remember that where there's a will there's a way! **Lows 3–5; 31** Try to set limits on yourself during this phase, even if you find this difficult.

FEBRUARY: Main Trends: 3–4 You should enjoy harmony in business, social and romantic relationships during this phase. Look to the co-operation of others to bring benefits. **5–6** Your social and romantic life may prove disappointing. Are you taking more than you give? **18–19** Seize the chance to catch up with any backlogs of work and get better organised, as this may give you the opportunity to get the best from both work and leisure. **Key Dates: Highs 12–14** Future career prospects look good – take advantage of your persuasive tongue, particularly when it comes to those in authority. **Lows 1; 27–28** You may struggle to make material progress or attract success, so concentrate on getting your strength back instead.

MARCH: Main Trends: 10–11 Take any opportunity to advance up the career ladder, with a little help from significant people – you'll never know until you try. **15–16** You may have the means to make major career changes with long-term benefits. Make the most of this and be prepared to take the leading role, but do avoid trying to dominate things. **20–21** Relationships should work out nicely and talks with others may prove highly inspiring. Look out for contacts with people who can put your ideas into practice! **Key Dates: Highs 8–9** There is the potential to be successful in your career – take advantage of your ability to get on well with others, particularly those in authority. **Lows 26–27** Success may be passing you by – keep a low profile and get plenty of rest and relaxation.

APRIL: Main Trends: 12–13 Capitalise on your charisma and ability to communicate. If you have creative interests, take any chance to expose your talents to the public eye. **19–20** This is the time to escape outmoded situations. Expect to feel a lot of pressure to make major decisions – don't be hurried, but don't dither too much either! **25–26** Communication may be lively and emotions too close to the surface. Prepare to use some tact. **Key Dates: Highs 8–9** Get busy – major endeavours should then go as planned, particularly as luck is on your side. **Lows 23–24** You may not be keen on taking risks and this is exactly how it should be!

MAY: Main Trends: 13–15 Seize any opportunities for intimate get-togethers, particularly while you are attuned to what your partner is thinking. **22–23** Make the most of any chance to be on the move and meet new people – you may make some inspiring contacts. **29–30** Emotional relationships may bring high drama and your material life may seem unsettled. This is the time to rid yourself of some deadwood. **Key Dates: Highs 5–7** Capitalise on your strong motivation and ability to spot opportunities from a distance. **Lows 20–21** You may lack energy and feel easily defeated by life, so avoid taking any silly risks.

Libra: tune into your lucky times

JUNE: Main Trends: 6–7 Personal relationships should be very cosy under this influence – an excellent time to talk over emotional issues and bare your soul. 14–15 There may be new social highlights on the horizon, so go all out to widen your horizons and introduce some culture into your life. 21–22 Focus on your potential for professional success. As things come to a head, it may be time for celebrations all round! **Key Dates: Highs** 2–3 Concentrate on making a start with new plans and schemes while you are streets ahead of the competition. **Lows** 16–18 Prepare yourself for setbacks while the control over certain situations is not within your hands.

JULY: Main Trends: 3–4 Capitalise on this boost to your personal self-confidence to bring success and recognition in your professional life. 5–6 This is the time to widen your horizons, through travel, learning or cultural input. 22–24 Communication is highlighted, so develop your negotiating skills and use your abilities to co-ordinate joint or team efforts. **Key Dates: Highs.** 26–27 Make the most of being able to get your own way and focus on major decisions while luck is on your side. **Lows** 14–15 You may struggle to make progress during this phase, so concentrate on recharging your batteries.

AUGUST: Main Trends: 1–3 While things are going well socially, exercise your diplomatic skills and express yourself in a refined way. Be open to new and exciting ideas. 21–22 You may feel you lack influence over your own life – concentrate on channelling your energies into other people's ambitions instead. 27–28 The pressure may be on professionally, but do you need to be in such a hurry to succeed? Avoid any trouble with those in authority. **Key Dates: Highs** 23–24 Push forth with new ideas at work and be sure to benefit from new initiatives. **Lows** 10–11 You may encounter opposition and struggle to achieve your objectives – get plenty of rest instead.

SEPTEMBER: Main Trends: 17–18 You may be easily influenced by other people and their ideas. Search out some solitude in order to function properly. Imaginative pursuits should go well. 21–22 You may be willing to sacrifice yourself for the ideal of love, but set limits on what you are prepared to do for others! 23–24 Make the most of your get up and go, and new projects should be successful. **Key Dates: Highs** 19–20 Seize any professional opportunities – you really can make your own luck! **Lows** 6–7 You may struggle to achieve results during this phase. Consider doing as little as possible.

OCTOBER: Main Trends: 10–11 Make the most of your lively mind to make an impact on the world, and look to diversity to bring success. 14–15 Love and romance are highlighted. Take advantage of this influence to attract goodwill. 23–24 Be sure to benefit from this positive focus on the physical side of life. Concentrate on consolidating recent objectives to bring material success. **Key Dates: Highs** 16–18 Use your natural business talent to work towards ambitious goals. **Lows** 3–4; 31 There could be setbacks in your career or social life, so focus on private matters and self-indulgence.

NOVEMBER: Main Trends: 8–9 Grasp any opportunities for monetary gain while most dealings should work in your favour. Look to financial partnerships for success. 16–17 Make the most of your strong personality and ability to win others over. 22–23 Concentrate on communication – listen out for new information in social situations. **Key Dates: Highs.** 13–14 Take a gamble and believe in yourself. Think positively and expect to win. **Lows** 1; 27–28 Keep life simple. Any overconfidence could be your undoing and you may lack patience.

DECEMBER: Main Trends: 1–3 Enjoy the complexity and variety of life. Focus on communication to learn something new that is to your advantage. 5–6 The past is highlighted so take a trip down memory lane and catch up with old friends. 21–22 Look to friends and family for strength and enjoyment. **Key Dates: Highs** 10–11 Positive thinking can bring great benefits during this phase – make the most of it. **Lows** 24–26 Prepare to feel challenged and don't expect much personal success at this time.

SCORPIO BORN PEOPLE
Birthdays: 24 October to 22 November inclusive
Planets: Mars, Pluto. Birthstone: Topaz. Lucky day: Tuesday

Keynote for the Year: *Look to your family and domestic life for fulfilment this year but, at the same time, be prepared to rethink friendships and wider social matters.*

JANUARY: Main Trends: 3–4 An influence favouring friendships and romantic involvements – make the most of the support you are offered and carefully cultivate useful contacts. **21–22** Again look to the home and family for invaluable support and a pleasant feeling of security. **23–24** Focus on communicating your ideas and impressing people in conversation and then watch for some interesting feedback. **Key Dates: Highs 18–20** A promising and rather hectic phase of personal satisfaction – capitalise on your luck. **Lows 6–7** Pace yourself during this lull when you may lack strength, and when results may be disappointing.

FEBRUARY: Main Trends: 4–5 Your work life is highlighted – focus on diplomacy and co-operation to get things done. **6–7** You may not be able to influence those at home, so prepare to toe the line, however much you may dislike this. **18–20** Love and romantic interests are enhanced, so sharpen up your personality and turn on those powers of attraction! **Key Dates: Highs 15–16** A time to be enterprising and outgoing, and possibly the leader, if not the centre, of any group. **Lows 2–3** You could get carried away under career pressure. Don't make mistakes you may later regret.

MARCH Main Trends: 8–9 Focus on creative and social issues to make life far more light hearted and romantic – get out to places of entertainment or hog the limelight! **16–17** Make the most of your improved self-esteem to win others over, but don't get too self-important. **20–21** Capitalise on your good mind for business, thinking along practical and conservative lines to come up with sound and productive ideas. **Key Dates: Highs 14–15** Take advantage of this positive influence to succeed in any form of physical or creative expression. Make the most of luck being on your side, too. **Lows 1–2; 28–30** Try to remain upbeat about life even if you can't live up to the expectations of others.

APRIL: Main Trends: 13–14 Look to your home and family to bring happiness. **19–20** Focus on social proceedings as things are looking more romantic and you may be more in demand than you thought. **22–23** A time of vitality in the workplace – channel this energy effectively, don't be in too much of a hurry and you should come out ahead. **Key Dates: Highs 10–12** With your winner mentality and faith in yourself, you can attract success! **Lows 25–26** You may feel that you can't do what you really want to do, so fulfil outstanding obligations and get some rest.

MAY: Main Trends: 13–14 Make the most of this phase during which relationships, both personal and professional, should function smoothly. Focus on business dealings to bring success. **20–21** This is a good time to get rid of situations that are past their best. Don't hang on to something just for the sake of it. **30–31** A lively period when the relationship balance may be tested – a partner shouldn't dominate your actions, nor you theirs. **Key Dates: Highs 8–9** Act quickly in order to achieve your aims during this phase. **Lows 22–23** Avoid heavy responsibilities as these may frustrate you while you are lacking in vitality. Take it easy!

JUNE: Main Trends: 6–7 All relationships are favourably highlighted – make the most of this trend towards romance. **14–15** Use this positive influence to keep the wheels of progress turning and accept the challenge to revitalise any elements of your life that aren't working out properly. **21–22** This is a great time to seek out the new and unusual – try to expand your personal world with new ideas, travel

Scorpio: a guide to your good-luck times

and a dash of culture! **Key Dates: Highs 4–5** You are in the driving seat where major plans are concerned. Give a hundred per cent and your efforts should be rewarded. **Lows 19–20** You may need a break from certain obligations – spend some time recharging your batteries.

JULY: Main Trends: 4–5 You can learn something new every day. Get out and about and put yourself in touch with the wider world. **6–7** Focus on a partnership, whether it be romantic or business, to bring improvements in your life. **22–23** Capitalise on your increased energies to get things done both at home and work. Concentrate on your career and enlisting valuable help. **Key Dates: Highs 1–3; 28–30** Take full advantage of this time of real innovation and a chance to make progress with your ambitions. **Lows 16–17** Don't take on too many commitments, but focus on essentials instead.

AUGUST: Main Trends: 1–3 This is a good time to be on the move. Make some unusual friendships and enjoy social activities to attract new ideas. **22–23** Focus on working n a group, and use your skills to mobilise team spirit. Be on the lookout for a brand new friendship. **27–28** Search out help in your career life and be prepared to use a little flattery to further your chances. **Key Dates: Highs 25–26** Think big and expect the best – you never know what is around the corner, especially under this influence. **Lows 12–13** Everyday life may refuse to work out right – you need to accept that you can't be in control of your destiny all of the time.

SEPTEMBER: Main Trends: 18–19 Focus on professional situations that offer variety and freedom of movement as these will enable you to use your ideas. **23–24** Capitalise on your ability to win friends and influence people and enjoy the input of colleagues who seem only to happy to help. **25–26** Prepare for setbacks and the lack of any immediate solution. Don't rely too much on a partner's support. Focus on the spiritual side of life to bring rewards. **Key Dates: Highs 21–22** This is an excellent period for getting initiatives off the ground. Look for help from unexpected sources. **Lows 8–10** Be prepared to make careful decisions and to go with the flow, especially if plans are delayed.

OCTOBER: Main Trends: 10–11 Concentrate on meditative pursuits – socialising has its time and place, but this isn't one of them! **14–16** Be prepared to take the rough with the smooth in relationships as loved ones may not be very responsive. **23–25** Make the most of this phase of increased self-confidence and dynamic action. By trusting in your intuitions, and having faith in your goals, you can create the optimal conditions for success. **Key Dates: Highs 19–20** Take advantage of your high energy levels to take on the world! **Lows 6–7** Think carefully about whether or not it is worth continuing with a plan of action that has become rather stranded.

NOVEMBER: Main Trends: 8–10 Look to a love interest to bring out the best in you and encourage you to be yourself. Focus on new affairs as these may prove long lasting. **17–18** Take advantage of your ability to make career decisions. It could even be a time to push your luck financially. **22–23** Practical and monetary matters are positively highlighted, so build on recent successes. Capitalise on your practical vision and common sense. **Key Dates: Highs 15–16** Make the most of your strong personal magnetism to influence others and get good results. **Lows 2–3; 29–30** Be prepared to experience self doubt and to feel disillusioned. Let it pass!

DECEMBER: Main Trends: 2–3 Be sure to benefit from this favourable time for business, when moves could lead to unexpected financial benefits, especially through the deliberations of a partner. **5–7** Stimulate the little grey cells. This is a good time for intellectual insights and improved communication – focus on gathering useful new information. **21–22** Another mental peak when you should use your mind to make clear choices and think things through in a successful way. **Key Dates: Highs 12–14** Make the most of this beneficial influence and you may see the culmination of a major project. **Lows 1; 27–28** Make lots of room for relaxation and leisure during this dispiriting influence.

SAGITTARIUS BORN PEOPLE
Birthdays: 23 November to 21 December inclusive
Planet: Jupiter. Birthstone: Turquoise. Lucky day: Thursday

Keynote for the Year: *Look to brand new studies or travel plans to bring success. Your professional life could bring new pressures, so don't overextend yourself.*

JANUARY: Main Trends: 3–4 Focus on the home and whatever is most familiar to bring pleasure – reunions with old colleagues could be just the thing. 19–20 Make the most of this highlight on communication and concentrate on what really matters during this busy phase. 23–24 A good time to build upon any recent promising starts – the keyword is security, so take steps to firm up your finances. **Key Dates: Highs** 21–22 Capitalise on your luck and the favourable conditions that should mean you can achieve your aims. **Lows** 8–9 Don't be overawed by what is going on outside and remember that you lack the potential for success.

FEBRUARY: Main Trends: 3–4 Make the most of your heightened powers of attraction and be prepared for your heart speaking louder than your head – in a good way! 4–5 Beware of a tendency to be argumentative. Don't let this make you unpopular or get others working against you! 20–21 Look to the domestic sphere and the past for fulfilment. **Key Dates; Highs** 17–19 Capitalise on your ability to make progress with any outstanding projects. Make the most of your luck too. **Lows** 5–6 This could prove a challenging period – think carefully about short-term decisions.

MARCH: Main Trends: 8–9 Focus on the home to bring pleasure into your life. Be on the lookout for extra support with a personal issue that has arisen recently. 14–15 Look for benefits on the domestic scene and enjoy re-living the good old days. 20–21 You should feel confident and dynamic, so use your charm to attract the goodwill of others and to achieve success. **Key Dates: Highs** 16–18 There could be a breakthrough with your ambitions and plans for the future – go for it! **Lows** 3–4; 31 There may not be much happening during this phase so take a break and save yourself both time and effort.

APRIL: Main Trends: 15–16 A good time for exchanging views – focus on working in a group, and get your ideas across successfully. 19–20 Bear in mind that progress at work could come more through who you know, rather than what you do. Make the most of the opportunity to relax professionally. 22–23 Channel your need to assert yourself into creative or romantic areas rather than just drawing attention to yourself! **Key Dates: Highs** 13–14 Take advantage of your ability to get what you want and look to those in authority to help get schemes off the ground. **Lows** 1; 27–28 You may lack enthusiasm, energy and luck, so keep your expectations simple.

MAY: Main Trends: 13–14 Make the most of this favourable time at work when things should move nicely towards their target. 20–21 Focus on joint dealings and social activities while your co-operative charm should make you popular with everyone. 30–31 A period of high energy – put your organisational abilities to use. You may be something of a perfectionist when completing tasks during this phase! **Key Dates: Highs** 10–12 Capitalise on your mental powers and infectious high spirits to get things going. **Lows** 24–25 There may be obstacles in the way of progress – take a slower approach and accept that things may not right themselves straight away.

JUNE: Main Trends: 1–2 Be prepared for changes to your prospects at work. Make a little effort and you may move further up the ladder of success. 13–14 Make the most of your social skills and enjoy the time spent with partners and colleagues – even those who may be new. 23–24 Take advantage of your emotional drive and put energy into improving your surroundings. Focus on the new things in life and take steps to get rid of the old. **Key Dates: Highs** 6–8 Take the opportunity to outdo the

Sagittarius: tune into your good-luck times

competition and get new endeavours up and running. **Lows 21–22** A planetary low point when you will require more rest than normal – take it easy.

JULY: Main Trends: 2–3 This is a good time to re-organise your affairs or rearrange your living situation. If sudden changes should happen, go with the flow. **22–23** Take any opportunities to broaden your social sphere and make valuable personal contacts through travel. You may find cultural issues rejuvenating. **24–25** Be on the lookout for mental stimulus and opportunities for personal freedom. Focus on widening your horizons in some way. **Key Dates: Highs 4–5** Make the most of this favourable time for formulating personal plans and getting support – seize the moment! **Lows 18–19** Life may be rather unstable and emotionally challenging, so take things easy.

AUGUST: Main Trends: 2–3 Look to emotional relationships for happiness and take the opportunity to gain valuable insight into what's on a partner's mind. **22–23** Your strengths should be in the ascendant, so plough your efforts into your career and professional matters. **26–27** Seize any opportunities for a change of scenery and take off somewhere exciting. Look to long journeys and new conversations to bring out the best in you. **Key Dates: Highs 27–29** This is a great time to get personal schemes underway – taking steps into the unknown could make a massive difference. **Lows 14–16** Beware overdoing things at work or being at cross purposes with others – this may lead to frustrations.

SEPTEMBER: Main Trends: 17–18 Focus on your career while you have the happy knack of doing the right thing at the right time! **20–21** Be sure to benefit from being in the professional spotlight – especially with regard to those in authority and what they have to offer. **22–23** Focus on your social life and any teamwork matters – things should go better in groups, whether at work or play. **Key Dates: Highs 23–25** Keep your eyes and ears open for useful knowledge and ideas – contact with professional people should be very beneficial. **Lows 11–12** You may struggle to organise yourself during this influence. Remain patient and let any chaos burn itself out.

OCTOBER: Main Trends: 10–11 Focus on your social life at this auspicious time by joining a group of some kind or making plans to meet others, whether new or old faces. **14–15** Concentrate on group dealings for maximum benefit while you function best in a team. **23–24** Beware of false optimism and don't promise anything you may not be able to deliver, or which you may want to back out of later. **Key Dates: Highs 21–22** Capitalise on your optimistic attitude and good fortune when it comes to both personal and professional goals. **Lows 8–9** Avoid taking unnecessary risks which could result in setbacks – this is not your most promising time.

NOVEMBER: Main Trends: 8–9 Beware of high-sounding ideas misleading you into making wrong decisions – a little more discrimination could be very valuable. **15–16** Listen out for useful information while your mind is sharp and you thrive on handling several different matters at once. **22–23** Make the most of your ability to command attention when you express your ideas. This can give you confidence and creative or leadership abilities. **Key Dates: Highs 17–19** Put your self-confidence and optimism to good use while you are feeling lucky and your expectations are high. **Lows 4–5** You may struggle to make progress, so avoid taking any major risks, and try to work within your limits.

DECEMBER: Main Trends: 4–5 Capitalise on your charm and refinement to attract the good life and all that's luxurious. **6–7** Focus on practical matters as these should result in success and even bring a little financial fortune your way. **21–22** Work to improve your finances while you have the capacity for monetary gain. **Key Dates: Highs 15–16** Another excellent time for making fresh starts of any kind – be prepared to burn the candle at both ends. **Lows 2–3; 29–30** Get plenty of rest and recharge your batteries before taking on any commitments. Suspend any important decisions.

CAPRICORN BORN PEOPLE
Birthdays: 22 December to 20 January inclusive
Planet: Saturn. Birthstone: Garnet. Lucky day: Saturday

Keynote for the Year: *Make the most of opportunities for material and financial gain, but consider abandoning certain outdated ideas and beliefs.*

JANUARY: Main Trends: 3–4 During this beneficial influence for relationships, enjoy casual conversation and make the most of your ability to appeal to people. **19–20** Make a little effort and you should be able to secure finances. Look to associations with people in important positions to bring success. **26–27** Focus on mental pursuits, the intellect and communication. This is a great time for conveying fresh ideas or being spontaneous. **Key Dates: Highs 23–25** A mental and physical peak – capitalise on your luck particularly where ambitious matters are concerned. **Lows 10–11** Make sure you're properly in the know before taking the initiative with important matters.

FEBRUARY: Main Trends: 2–3 Stick to a familiar environment in order to thrive. This is a good time for revisiting the past. **4–5** You can thrive in the practical sphere. Focus on whatever is new and challenging, but avoid reckless decisions! **18–19** Capitalise on your ability to communicate effectively with both friends and colleagues, and be on the lookout for important information that is crucial to your plans. **Key Dates: Highs 20–21** Make the most of your powers of attraction and look out for exciting new experiences. **Lows 6–7** You may not feel fantastic, so prepare for a lack of progress.

MARCH: Main Trends: 8–9 Capitalise on your curiosity and ability to communicate by focusing on discussion, dialogue and new subjects of any kind. **15–16** Your attitude may bring out a competitive approach in others, which could lead to conflict, so try to avoid needless arguments. **21–22** Make the most of this influence to create a pleasant environment at home and benefit emotionally from the company of family and friends. **Key Dates: Highs 19–20** Be sure to benefit from your high mental energy levels by enjoying lots of variety and changing the pace of life. **Lows 5–7** This is a sluggish time when you should watch out for pitfalls on the road to progress.

APRIL: Main Trends: 12–13 The good things in life may come easily to you – make the effort and you may get what you need just when you need it! **19–20** Capitalise on your ability to win the affections and confidence of others and to make life more fun and romantic. **22–23** Your strong emotional energy could produce harsh words at home. Use this energy to make improvements to where you live and to talk things through reasonably. **Key Dates: Highs 15–17** Make the most of any opportunities that arise and use your optimism to attract success. **Lows 2–3; 29–30** Think hard about whether you are doing the right thing – it may be wiser to put certain issues on hold.

MAY: Main Trends: 15–16 Look to others for confidence as you seek to be yourself. Concentrate on creating a pleasing impression on others. **20–21** This is a good time to throw yourself into work and undertake new tasks in the practical sphere. **30–31** Beware of taking everything personally while you have strong feelings of self-worth. Your competitive instincts are aroused, especially in love and romance – try to play it cool! **Key Dates: Highs 13–14** Focus on professional ambitions while you are full of energy and feel on the top of the world. **Lows 26–27** Prepare for a period of change in your life during which you may lack energy and feel limited by circumstance.

JUNE: Main Trends: 6–7 Look to romance and matters of the heart to bring fulfilment. You will expect to be noticed and appreciated – and are probably right to do so! **14–15** Focus on practical ideas and work-related issues during this industrious phase. **21–22** Concentrate on social matters and

Capricorn: plan your life into your good-luck days

relationships while these have lots to offer. Bear in mind that you may lack individual ambition. **Key Dates: Highs 9–10** Take advantage of luck being on your side to move towards your goals. **Lows 23–24** You are unlikely to make much progress, but don't be too discouraged.

JULY: Main Trends: 3–4 Look to partnerships with other people for fun and profit – keep your eyes and ears open for input, news and information. **14–16** Make the most of who you know and some valuable help to make progress at work! **22–23** Capitalise on your power to effect positive change and be prepared to put something in the past for good. **Key Dates: Highs 6–8** Be ready to act upon any new opportunities during this positive phase. **Lows 20–21** Be as straightforward as possible in your dealings with others, especially business partners and those in authority.

AUGUST: Main Trends: 5–6 Focus on relationships while you are likely to be appreciated, and capitalise on your diplomatic skills to deal with those in disagreement. **22–23** Go with the urge to widen both your intellectual and geographical horizons. **26–28** Be prepared for intimate relationships taking on more emotional significance. Make the most of this beneficial phase for money-making partnerships. **Key Dates: Highs 2–4** Capitalise on your self-assurance and seize any opportunities to improve on your current position. **Lows 17–18** Conflicts could flare up because of impatience when dealing with setbacks. Try to keep things on an even keel.

SEPTEMBER: Main Trends: 18–19 You may have a low boredom threshold, so stay at the forefront of the action and keep some variety in your life. **20–21** Grasp any opportunity to get away from it all through extended study or travel. Try out some new interests. **22–24** Work should improve and those in authority should be supportive of your ideas. Make the most of this to attract success! **Key Dates: Highs 26–27** This is a good time to expand your interests whatever you happen to be doing. Be sure to profit from favourable business contacts. **Lows 13–14** Try to remain objective while there is confusion and even the best laid plans fall flat.

OCTOBER: Main Trends: 12–13 A rather ambitious period when it comes to career matters – capitalise on your natural instinct for making the right move at the right time. **14–16** Your professional life should be making you feel optimistic. Look to fortunate contacts to boost your future plans. **26–27** Teamwork and social-based matters are positively highlighted. Focus on activities with groups and organisations, or entertainment with friends. **Key Dates: Highs 23–25** Make the most of high-minded ambitions in order to get ahead. **Lows 10–11** You may struggle to put in the effort – consider putting plans to one side.

NOVEMBER: Main Trends: 8–9 A great time to throw in your lot with others – look to your social life and teamwork for your most rewarding moments. **16–17** Focus on your inner life while there are only few ways to get ahead. Take your time at work and don't succumb to any pressures. **22–23** This is the time to take stock of what you've accomplished in life so far and be less concerned with your ambitions. **Key Dates: Highs 20–21** Apply your intuitive insight and original thinking to creative enterprises, and look to influential people for support. **Lows 6–7** Personal difficulties may come to a head – talk things over with a partner.

DECEMBER: Main Trends: 1–2 Your love life may be in the doldrums. Look to dealings with others to gain insights, but don't ignore your own goals. **5–6** Take advantage of this mental peak and a more light-hearted influence to bring charisma to your daily dealings and attract some new admirers. **21–22** The sun occupying your sign enhances your powers of personality and the need to be number one. Capitalise on this dynamic period to carry things off with flair. **Key Dates: Highs 17–18** Make the most of your confidence about life and the fact that certain decisions have rather lucky results. **Lows: 4–5; 31** As the pace of life slows down, don't try to force any issues.

AQUARIUS BORN PEOPLE
Birthdays: 21 January to 19 February inclusive
Planets: Saturn, Uranus. Birthstone: Amethyst. Lucky day: Saturday

Keynote for the Year: *With lucky Jupiter in your sign, this may be a year for fresh starts of any kind – be prepared for opportunity to knock, but eliminate life's non-essentials at the same time.*

JANUARY: Main Trends: 3–4 Plan properly and make the most of your natural talent for attracting the finer things of the material world. **19–20** Take the leading role in professional matters while you are personable and noticeable. **21–22** Take care as communication matters can cause problems and not everything you hear is to be believed. **Key Dates: Highs 26–27** Trust your instincts and make the most of your luck during this unexpected boost. **Lows 12–13** Keep a low profile while your ideas may be impractical and hasty decisions have the potential to disrupt work routines.

FEBRUARY: Main Trends: 2–3 You know how important first impressions are, so use your natural charm to win over others. **4–5** With Mars in your sign, you should capitalise on your get-up-and-go mood. Get some physical exercise or take an adventurous trip, and don't be held back by anything! **18–19** Capitalise on your ability to make money, field ideas and attract success. Slow and steady is the way forward. **Key Dates: Highs 22–24** Don't be afraid to be ambitious during this personal high – focus on important long-range aspirations. **Lows 8–9** Beware of demanding what you want as this could lead to setbacks and frustrations. Don't expect your energy to last.

MARCH: Main Trends: 10–11 Make the most of your good head for business to come up with sound and productive ideas that may prove profitable. **15–16** You should thrive by being independent in the practical sphere and in the pursuit of money. You're not best placed to take orders! **24–25** Seize any opportunities for variety and mental stimulus – short journeys or new input, whatever develops your mind and keeps you interested. **Key Dates: Highs 21–23** Capitalise on this high when you should be able to make progress, and may even achieve overnight success through creative and original ideas. **Lows 8–9** Play it safe at this time when you may struggle to get things done.

APRIL: Main Trends: 12–14 Make the most of the potential for new romance as all kinds of personal relationships are enhanced. **20–21** Focus on activities at home for entertainment and consider taking a journey into the past. **22–23** Beware being over-optimistic regarding future possibilities – try to stay focused and to curb any outspoken tendencies. **Key Dates: Highs 18–19** Show a bit of initiative and new ideas, change and personal growth are all possible. **Lows 4–5** Don't undertake unrealistic tasks as you may have to jettison them and start over again later.

MAY: Main Trends: 13–14 Make this a phase of positive changes at home while the domestic scene is far more busy and active than usual. **20–21** Romantic matters should see you taking the starring role – focus on places of entertainment or intimate twosomes. **30–31** You may prove a little dominating at home and relationships may become strained. To achieve harmony, try to live and let live. **Key Dates: Highs 15–16** Make the most of your ability to get what you want from a certain amount of wheeling and dealing. **Lows 1–2; 28–29** There may be sudden and unexpected setbacks. Avoid any hazards and promising more than you can deliver.

JUNE: Main Trends: 6–7 Domestic conditions should to be at their best. Family and friends and the past should put a smile on your face, so it's a great time for entertaining at home. **14–15** Grasp any opportunities to impress others with your overtures. Be sure to benefit from being in the limelight and from this auspicious time for romance. **21–22** Focus on possible gains through work and the practical world. Be open to advice from others, such as colleagues and bosses. **Key Dates: Highs 11–13** Be sure

Aquarius: tune into your favourable days

to take full advantage of any situations that you find yourself in. **Lows 25–26** Prepare to face new obligations and restraints that may deny you freedom.

JULY: Main Trends: 3–4 Real accomplishment is possible – look for signposts to career success. **5–6** Take advantage of this beneficial influence for your love life during which a new relationship should prove inspiring and existing ones will flourish. **24–25** You should work well in conjunction with others. Reap the rewards of more give and take in personal and business relationships, whether personal or business. **Key Dates: Highs 9–10** Capitalise on your powers of persuasion and ability to put your point of view across. **Lows 22–23** You may struggle to progress and lack patience – beware minor conflicts with others.

AUGUST: Main Trends: 1–3 Be sure to benefit from professional relationships, particularly those with people who are in a position of authority. **22–23** Look to the help of a loved one to make necessary changes in your personal life – you may even find monetary assistance if this is required. **26–27** A beneficial social influence when you should look to meeting new people and personal relationships for enjoyment. **Key Dates: Highs 5–6** Capitalise on your persuasive powers to get your own way – time to have that talk with the boss! **Lows: 19–20** Persevere, but with caution. Don't waste time on matters that refuse to budge.

SEPTEMBER: Main Trends: 18–19 Certain matters you have outgrown may start to fade away – take the opportunity to replace and renew. **20–21** Look to close emotional involvements for enjoyment. This is a good period for joint anything, especially shared feelings and money. **23–24** Be willing to expand your philosophical horizons. Use your tolerant, broad-minded approach to get the best from life. **Key Dates: Highs 1; 28–30** Take advantage of your ability to make major decisions at this time of good fortune. **Lows 15–16** Prepare for an unproductive phase when you may lack energy and your over-confidence may lead to minor setbacks.

OCTOBER: Main Trends: 10–11 Look to a variety of interests to deal with your sense of restlessness. Make the most of your acute mind to make decisions at speed. **14–15** Look to intellectual talks and discussion, or just getting happily lost in a conversation, to bring benefits. **23–24** Aim high during this important period when there is a lot at stake. You may have to take on a key role career-wise. **Key Dates: Highs 26–27** Be sure to benefit while professional matters are almost tailor-made for you. Look to those in authority for invaluable support. **Lows 12–13** You may be disenchanted with life – take a sabbatical and shelve ambitions for a while.

NOVEMBER Main Trends: 11–12 You can bring an atmosphere of harmony to the professional sphere – capitalise on this to get your own way and to get others to help you. **16–17** Focus on groups, and exciting things should happen. Make use of your persuasive charms to galvanise others into action. **25–26** Concentrate on group-related activities. You should gain from helping others and can be counted on to be a good team-player. **Key Dates: Highs 22–24** Make the most of your increased physical energy during this robust period. This is the time to start new projects. **Lows 8–10** While conditions may be rather taxing, keep things simple and unambitious.

DECEMBER: Main Trends: 1–2 Social matters are highlighted – look to groups where you should find it easy to make a good impression. **8–9** This is a period for reflection, and learning from your mistakes. Try to avoid misunderstandings that may arise through communication. **22–23** This influence is characterised by a sense of isolation. Spend some time alone and focus on working behind the scenes in order to achieve success. **Key Dates: Highs 19–21** Make the most of your drive to succeed and some sheer good luck to see real accomplishment. **Lows 6–7** Beware of deceiving yourself and be careful whom you trust – avoid anyone who sounds too good to be true.

PISCES BORN PEOPLE
Birthdays: 20 February to 20 March inclusive
Planets: Jupiter, Neptune. Birthstone: Bloodstone. Lucky day: Thursday

Keynote for the Year: *Look to personal and emotional matters for a real sense of inner security, but be prepared to sort the wheat from the chaff in your social life.*

JANUARY: Main Trends: 3–4 You can be a winner in love while your social and romantic life is highlighted – get out there and meet some new people. **19–20** Focus on your inner world, and new ideas should start to emerge. **21–22** While you are an excellent catalyst for getting people together, concentrate on group-related matters. Listen out for some useful information from a friend. **Key Dates: Highs 28–30** This is a good period for developing your ambitions – look to those around you to offer support and goodwill. **Lows: 14–15** While you find circumstances are going against you and serious issues are coming to the fore, try to work through things patiently.

FEBRUARY: Main Trends: 3–4 This is a good time for learning new things – keep your mind open to inventive ideas and look out for people to share them with! **5–6** You may encounter obstacles in your daily life. Take a more careful and considered approach to your plans. **18–19** Make the most of your considerable ambition and drive to make good things happen, both personally and professionally, and to improve your overall circumstances. **Key Dates: Highs 25–26** The moves you make may well be inspired. Take advantage of this to make your hopes and dreams more of a reality. **Lows 10–11** Don't push yourself too hard – relax and enjoy life!

MARCH: Main Trends: 8–9 Keep your eyes and ears open for some significant new input – and look out for some exciting or inspiring people. **15–16** Energy levels are high, so be bold and do the right thing, even if the changes you want to make may be challenged. **20–21** Take advantage of any recent developments at work and consolidate any material gains you have made. Make an early start and put money-making ideas into action. **Key Dates: Highs 24–25** Take advantage of your physical vitality to get on with current plans and schemes. **Lows 10–11** Things have a tendency to go wrong; don't expect too much from life as this may result in dissatisfaction.

APRIL: Main Trends: 12–13 While your strengths are limited, don't go in for grandiose ideas. Look to private matters for enjoyment. **19–20** Communication of any kind is highlighted. Make use of your original ideas and insights to advance your plans. **23–24** Give careful consideration to a monetary pursuit and avoid any financial extravagance as you may come to regret it later. **Key Dates: Highs 20–22** There is nothing you cannot accomplish if you really want it – strike while the iron is hot. **Lows 6–7** Expect challenges in your career, and make the most of your self-discipline to bring success.

MAY: Main Trends: 13–14 Take advantage of this mental high when information is flowing nicely – listen out for some marvellous advice that could save a lot of trouble later. **20–21** Look to the familiarity of your home and family for happiness and reassurance. **30–31** Your thinking is quick and your speech to the point, but you should play down the assertive and egomaniac sides to your nature. **Key Dates: Highs 18–19** This is the time to take chances with life and be a little unconventional – success could be yours for the taking. **Lows 3–4; 30–31** Prepare to contend with disagreements in your personal life during this phase.

JUNE: Main Trends: 6–7 Make the most of your ability to communicate and get along with others, and be aware that your opinions could have a considerable influence. **17–18** Loved ones at home

Pisces: make the most of your good-luck times

know how to bring out the best in you – look to them to make life secure and rewarding. **21–22** Enjoy this extended period of socialising, fun and romance as personal relationships improve – you may find you're the star attraction. **Key Dates: Highs 14–15** Have faith in the future and take a gamble to enhance your chances of success. **Lows 1; 27–28** Be easy on yourself if you lack enthusiasm and energy or just feel out of sorts.

JULY: Main Trends: 3–5 Make the most of your charm and charisma to enrich your relationships – you shouldn't have to try too hard with friends or loved ones! **5–6** Focus on the domestic scene and the past to find fulfilment. Why not call up an old friend you haven't seen for ages? **22–23** You could be making strides in your work life, so look out for offers of various kinds coming your way. **Key Dates: Highs 11–13** Capitalise on your considerable personal influence and luck. **Lows 24–25** A planetary lull – this is not a good time for initiating any major sort of change.

AUGUST: Main Trends: 1–2 Emotional relationships and romantic affairs are highlighted, so take the time to nurture them. Focus on intimate twosomes. **23–24** Search out a wider circle of social contacts. Get out and meet new people and even new romantic interests. **26–27** Make the most of your productivity and self-confidence at work – it may lead to the successful culmination of an ambitious project. **Key Dates: Highs 7–9** Try out your luck and you should be able to reap the benefit of all the efforts you have made lately. **Lows 21–22** You may be in the dark over an important matter – be patient and don't take any risky decisions.

SEPTEMBER: Main Trends: 19–20 Reap the rewards of your outgoing nature and skill in handling others – you'll probably find out just how popular you are. **20–21** Assume a high social profile to attract a new love life while relationships are enhanced. **24–25** Don't get stuck in a rut with recent interests during this period of renewal and regeneration, especially if abandoning them makes more sense. **Key Dates: Highs 4–5** People with influence may be able to guide you towards success, so don't be afraid to seek out their help. **Lows 17–18** Try to meet obstacles with patience and forethought rather than compulsive acts, otherwise just rest up as much as possible.

OCTOBER: Main Trends: 10–11 Prepare for people and things you have grown used to and based your security on slipping away. Let them go and look ahead to the future. **16–17** Capitalise on your ability to make vital changes to your life. Grasp joint financial opportunities as they could be rewarding in the long term. **23–25** Satisfy your yearning for fresh fields with travel and intellectual studies or discussion. You need something more imaginative and less mundane. **Key Dates: Highs 1; 28–30** Take advantage of your good fortune to bring an important project to a head. **Lows 14–15** Avoid scattering your energies on pointless tasks in the face of setbacks.

NOVEMBER: Main Trends: 8–9 Focus on meeting people and extended travel to direct your attention to the outside world. **16–18** Capitalise on your confidence to take on new initiatives during this favourable time for your career and for business expansion. **22–23** Start new projects or push forward with those already in motion. This is a good time professionally and you have plenty of ambition. **Key Dates: Highs 25–26** This is a great period for putting big ideas into practice – the bigger the idea, the better! **Lows 11–12** As obstacles slow you down, consider a more cautious approach.

DECEMBER: Main Trends: 1–3 Take advantage of your considerable personal charm and influence to get ahead professionally and to attract the goodwill of others. **5–6** Focus on entertaining new ideas, travel and meeting different kinds of people during this beneficial influence. **20–21** Look to large gatherings to get the best from both your social and work life – or even both. **Key Dates: Highs 22–23** Make the most of your special talent for attracting luck or garnering the power of positive thinking to your benefit! **Lows 8–9** Keep a lid on grandiose plans and ambitions, as good luck is not on your side.

Pinpoint your special days with Old Moore

200-year Perpetual Calendar

Do you know on which day of the week you or your friends were born? You may remember that World War II was declared on Sunday, 3 September 1939, but on which day did World War I start?

This calendar, created originally by C. E. Forsythe, allows you to find the weekday for any date from 1850 to 2050. You will find it useful and informative and very simple to use. Just follow the instructions to check birthdays, events and special occasions.

- Find the year in Table A.
- Follow across on the same line to Table B and select the number under the relevant month.
- Add this number to the date.
- Look up this number in Table C and follow across to the left to find the day of the week.

Table B

	Jan	Feb	Mar	Apri	May	June	July	Aug	Sept	Oct	Nov	Dec

Table A

								Jan	Feb	Mar	Apri	May	June	July	Aug	Sept	Oct	Nov	Dec
1850	1878		1918	1946	1974	2002	2030	2	5	5	1	3	6	1	4	0	2	5	0
1851	1879		1919	1947	1975	2003	2031	3	6	6	2	4	0	2	5	1	3	6	1
*1852	1880		1920	1848	1976	2004	2032	4	0	1	4	6	2	4	0	3	5	1	3
1853	1881		1921	1949	1977	2005	2033	6	2	2	5	0	3	5	1	4	6	2	4
1854	1882		1922	1950	1978	2006	2034	0	3	3	6	1	4	6	2	5	0	3	5
1855	1883		1923	1951	1979	2007	2035	1	4	4	0	2	5	0	3	6	1	4	6
*1856	1884		1924	1952	1980	2008	2036	2	5	6	2	4	0	2	5	1	3	6	1
1857	1885		1925	1953	1981	2009	2037	4	0	0	3	5	1	3	6	2	4	0	2
1858	1886		1926	1954	1982	2010	2038	5	1	1	4	6	2	4	0	3	5	1	3
1859	1887		1927	1955	1983	2011	2039	6	2	2	5	0	3	5	1	4	6	2	4
*1860	1888		1928	1956	1984	2012	2040	0	3	4	0	2	5	0	3	6	1	4	6
1861	1889	1901	1929	1957	1985	2013	2041	2	5	5	1	3	6	1	4	0	2	5	0
1862	1890	1902	1930	1958	1986	2014	2042	3	6	6	2	4	0	2	5	1	3	6	1
1863	1891	1903	1931	1959	1987	2015	2043	4	0	0	3	5	1	3	6	2	4	0	2
*1864	1892	1904	1932	1960	1988	2016	2044	5	1	2	5	0	3	5	1	4	6	2	4
1865	1893	1905	1933	1961	1989	2017	2045	0	3	3	6	1	4	6	2	5	0	3	5
1866	1894	1906	1934	1962	1990	2018	2046	1	4	4	0	2	5	0	3	6	1	4	6
1867	1895	1907	1935	1963	1991	2019	2047	2	5	5	1	3	6	1	4	0	2	5	0
*1868	1896	1908	1936	1964	1992	2020	2048	3	6	0	3	5	1	3	6	2	4	0	2
1869	1897	1909	1937	1965	1993	2021	2049	5	1	1	4	6	2	4	0	3	5	1	3
1870	1898	1910	1938	1966	1994	2022	2050	6	2	2	5	0	3	5	1	4	6	2	4
1871	1899	1911	1939	1967	1995	2023		0	3	3	6	1	4	6	2	5	0	3	5
*1872		1912	1940	1968	1996	2024		1	4	5	1	3	6	1	4	0	2	5	0
1873		1913	1941	1969	1997	2025		3	6	6	2	4	0	2	5	1	3	6	1
1874		1914	1942	1970	1998	2026		4	0	0	3	5	1	3	6	2	4	0	2
1875		1915	1943	1971	1999	2027		5	1	1	4	6	2	4	0	3	5	1	3
*1876		1916	1944	1972	2000	2028		6	2	3	6	1	4	6	2	5	0	3	5
1877	1900	1917	1945	1973	2001	2029		1	4	4	0	2	5	0	3	6	1	4	6

Table C

Sunday	1	8	15	22	29	36
Monday	2	9	16	23	30	37
Tuesday	3	10	17	24	31	
Wednesday	4	11	18	25	32	
Thursday	5	12	19	26	33	
Friday	6	13	20	27	34	
Saturday	7	14	21	28	35	

Example: 3 March 1896
March 1896 = 0
Date = 3
0 + 3 = 3 so it fell on a Tuesday

Example: 27 July 2005
July 2005 = 5
Date = 27
5 + 27 = 32 so it will fall on a Wednesday

* Years on the lines to the right of the asterisks are leap years.

Gardening by the Moon

In the second century AD, the astronomer Claudius Ptolemy reported of the practical, hard-headed farmers of the Roman Empire that they *'notice the aspects of the Moon, when at full, in order to direct the copulation of their herds and flocks, and the setting of plants or sowing of seeds; and there is not an individual who considers these general precautions as impossible or unprofitable.'*

The idea that the Moon exerts an influence on plant growth is as old as agriculture and embedded in the folklore of many societies. I became intrigued when working on a bio-dynamic farm and decided to investigate the evidence.

The effect of sowing date on crop yield has been thoroughly investigated by the bio-dynamic movement. For some decades, Maria Thun has reported annual results that show yields varying in accordance with the sidereal zodiac. Recent experiments have shown that the metabolism of plants, indicated by such things as their water absorption or oxygen metabolism, responds considerably to the lunar cycle. University of Paris researchers have demonstrated that plant DNA changes in tune with this cycle. Trees are surrounded by measurable electric fields, monitored for years by Ralph Markson in the US, that demonstrate distinctly lunar rhythms. My own experiments with seeds confirm the results published by Kolisko in the late 1930s and the John Innes Foundation around 1940, that seeds usually germinate better if sown around the Full Moon, and especially on the previous day or two.

Animals coming on heat is also cyclic and traditions link their fertility to the lunar cycle. Data from a thoroughbred stud farm clearly shows both increased fertility and increased coming-on-heat on the days around and just after the Full Moon.

Keys to understanding the relationship of plant response to lunar influence have now emerged and can be incorporated into a gardener's plans as to when best to carry out various tasks. For example, the waning half of the lunar month is best for pruning trees, while the waxing half is better for grafting.

Crops also belong to one of the elements: Earth (Root), Water (Leaf), Air (Flower) or Fire (Fruit-seed). From this it follows that there is a lunar timetable appropriate for each crop. For instance, potatoes, as a Root-crop, grow best when they are sown as the Moon is passing in front of Earth-element constellations.

My book, *Gardening and Planting by the Moon* (see page 69), is an invitation to gardeners to investigate the cycles of plant growth, a synthesis of time-honoured traditions and modern research. Totally practical – you need no scientific knowledge – it offers clear explanations followed by a daily calendar outlining the gardening tasks you should focus on to achieve the best results. I hope that this manual will be used for its practical advantages and as an inspiration to gardeners to become more aware of the life-rhythms in nature which mysteriously connect the growth of plants with cosmic time-cycles.

Nick Kollerstrom

Angler's Guide for 2009
THE BEST DATES AND TECHNIQUES FOR SUCCESSFUL FISHING

JANUARY: Sport can be hard due to low temperatures, so stick to deeper water on rivers and lakes. Backwaters are a good bet when main rivers are flooded; try float or leger tactics in slack water swims. Flounder anglers will find best sport in the south-west estuaries, hotly tipped to produce a record specimen. Codling still available on beaches but will soon thin out. **Best days:** 1, 2 (am), 9 (pm), 10, 11 (am), 18, 19, 20 (am), 28, 29, 30 (am).

FEBRUARY: Predator fishing offers the best action with pike, perch and zander all possible on fish baits, but scale down your tackle if the temperature plummets. Big chub can also be had on leger tactics. Spring salmon on the cards for game anglers, but beach rods will have to work harder for their catches. Flatties will still feature, although bigger fish can be had when afloat. **Best days:** 6, 7, 14 (pm), 15, 16, 24 (pm), 25, 26.

MARCH: The freshwater river season closes on the 14th, but almost all commercial still waters will stay open. If mild weather comes early, head for sheltered lakes which can produce superb mixed catches of roach, bream, carp and even tench. Trout anglers head for deep, still waters from the 15th. **Best days:** 5 (pm), 6, 7 (am), 14, 15, 24, 25, 26 (am).

APRIL: Beach anglers can enjoy the spring run of codling, while those fishing wrecks can expect bumper hauls of pollack, ling and occasional big cod on artificial baits. Ray fishing good, especially in the Solent. Most flies will take trout on still waters but a more careful approach is needed in rivers. **Best days:** 1 (pm), 2, 3, 10 (pm), 11, 12, 20, 21, 22 (am), 28, 29, 30.

MAY: Crab baits worthy for early school bass, flounder and eel, while ragworm and lugworm will take their fair share of plaice in harbours and estuaries. Still-water trout should respond to warmer weather and can be taken on floating lines. Carp will be the bulk of catches for commercial still-water anglers. **Best days:** 7 (pm), 8, 9, 17 (pm), 18, 19 (am), 26, 27, 28 (am).

JUNE: The Glorious 16th will enable specimen tench, carp and bream to be targeted with big baits on both float and leger tackle. Rivers with more pace should provide excellent catches of roach and chub. Beach anglers will find bass more widespread, while their boat counterparts can expect mackerel – the perfect bait for shark and tope, which will start to show off many southern and Welsh ports. **Best days:** 4, 5, 6 (am), 14, 15, 16 (am), 22 (pm), 23, 24 (am).

JULY: Top sport on rivers and lakes with virtually all species responsive, mostly to particle baits such as corn, hemp and tares. Try swims with plenty of flow as fish, particularly barbel and bream, will be hungry for oxygen-rich water during hot weather. Evening sessions ideal for fly anglers pursuing trout. Shy mullet may be tempted during quiet days around harbours, and bass will be bigger. **Best days:** 1, 2, 3 (am), 11, 12, 13 (am), 20, 21, 22 (am), 28, 29, 30 (am).

AUGUST: Low oxygen levels suggest fishing either very early morning or evening periods. Sea anglers afloat can look forward to a multitude of species including bream, bass, pollack, conger and gurnard. Fresh fish baits and crab will outscore all others. **Best days:** 7 (pm), 8, 9 (am), 16 (pm), 17, 18 (am), 24 (pm), 25, 26, 27 (am).

SEPTEMBER: Fish will have had time to feed well and big specimens can be expected. Barbel, roach, bream, tench and chub will all be at their optimum weight. Trout anglers may struggle to locate decent fish, although beach and boat rods will be hunting big bass with sand eel baits, crab or lures. **Best days:** 3 (pm), 4, 5, 6 (am), 13, 14, 15 (am), 21, 22, 23 (am).

OCTOBER: Cooler temperatures may mean slow sport on lakes, but rivers will be at their peak for roach, chub and dace on caster or maggot. Float tactics are good but don't discount leger or feeder gear. Beach anglers expect the first of the winter codling, where lugworm and squid will be top baits. Extra water may prompt decent catches of salmon for game anglers. **Best days:** 1, 2, 3 (am), 10, 11, 12 (am), 28, 29, 30 (am).

NOVEMBER: With shorter days, codling will come closer inshore, especially at deeper venues such as steep beaches, harbour walls and piers. Bad weather may mean slower sport for coarse anglers, who need to scale down hooks and baits. Predator hunters can expect big pike on baits rather than lures. **Best days:** 6, 7, 8 (am), 15, 16, 24 (pm), 25, 26, 27 (am).

DECEMBER: A roving approach is best during colder weather. Try different swims on backwaters, where roach will take bread flake, and chub can be had on cheese paste, bread, worms and cockles. Pin baits hard to the bottom or let them roll in the flow. After a storm is ideal for targeting codling on beaches, when they attack food stirred up by rough weather. Try night sessions for greater success. **Best days:** 3 (pm), 4, 5 (am), 12 (pm), 13, 14 (am), 22, 23, 24 (am), 31st.

Please name FOULSHAM'S ALMANACK when replying to advertisers

Suddenly My Memory Failed Me!

A FAMOUS international publisher reports that there is a simple technique for acquiring a powerful memory which can pay you real dividends in both business and social advancement. It works like magic to give you added poise, self-confidence and greater popularity.

INSTANT RECALL

According to this publisher, you need never forget another appointment — ever! You can learn names, faces, facts and figures faster than you ever thought possible. You could be able to imprint whole books on your memory after a single reading. You may be more successful in your studies and examinations. At parties and dinners you need never again be at a loss for appropriate words or entertaining stories. In fact, you could be more poised and self-confident in everything you say and do.

FREE INFORMATION PACK

Full details of this simple, self-training method for developing skill in remembering have been printed in a fascinating information pack, sent free on request. No obligation. Just phone 0800 298 7070 free, complete and return the coupon below (no stamp is needed if posted in the U.K.), send an e-mail (see coupon), visit our website at www.firstclassmemory.com or send your name and address to: Memory and Concentration Studies, FREEPOST OMM18T, Marple, Stockport, Cheshire SK6 6YA **TODAY**.

To: Memory and Concentration Studies, FREEPOST OMM18T, Stockport, Cheshire SK6 6YA.

Please send me your free Memory information pack..

NAME...
(Mr / Mrs / Miss /Ms)
ADDRESS ....
....
....Postcode.....................

Post TODAY, call 0800 298 7070 FREE or visit our website at www.firstclassmemory.com
E-mail: OMM18E@firstclassmemory.com with your name and address

---

Need a little extra HELP?

Let me help **you**, as I have thousands of others since 1954. Simply send me your Full Name, Address and Date of Birth together with a couple of <u>loose</u> stamps to help with postage and I will send you **FREE** of charge your **'Zodiac Star Reading'** together with details of how I can make your predictions and directions for the FULL Twelve months ahead, a most successful **Lucky Numbers System** and **YOUR very own Golden-Key** to the future.

Make sure you are in the best position to take advantage of every opportunity the future has to offer.

Write **NOW**, remember you have nothing to lose but **everything** to gain.

𝒦atrina

Est. 1954

𝒦atrina
Britain's favourite Astrologer

(Studio OM9) PO Box 507, Enfield, Middlesex EN2 7ZP

Make the most of your garden in 2009

Best Sowing and Planting Times for the Garden in 2009

WHEN TO PLANT OR SOW BY THE MOON TO GET THE BEST RESULTS

Peas, beans, flowering vegetables and plants which produce fruit above the ground should always be sown when the Moon is going to the full. Potatoes and root crops should always be sown when the Moon is low and below the Earth. If you sow, plant or re-pot at the times set out below, it is reasonably certain you will have really fine results. The times are Greenwich Mean Time. Allowances must be made for British Summer Time.

Month	Day	Planting Times		
JANUARY	10, 11, 12 25, 26, 27	9.20 am to 11.30 am 9.00 am to 11.55 am	12.50 to 3.05 pm 1.30 to 3.25 pm	
FEBRUARY	8, 9, 10 24, 25, 26	9.10 am to 11.15 am 8.55 am to 11.00 am	12.40 to 2.30 pm 12.15 to 2.10 pm	3.30 to 4.10 pm 3.20 to 4.25 pm
		Continue to sow peas, beans, onions, spinach, savoys, lettuce, celery, cauliflowers, carrots, parsnips and radishes. Cut early kidney potatoes for seed and put them in a stove or hotbed to start them for planting out.		
MARCH	10, 11, 12 25, 26, 27	8.20 am to 10.50 pm 8.05 am to 10.35 pm	12.00 to 2.20 pm 11.50 to 2.45 pm	3.10 to 4.45 pm 3.15 to 5.15 pm
		Vegetables should be put into the ground this month. Sow asparagus, celery, cauliflower, broccoli, spinach, onions, carrots, peas, beans, savoy, parsnips, radishes, etc. Plant red cabbage and sea-kale.		
APRIL	8, 9, 10 24, 25, 26	7.50 am to 11.10 am 7.40 am to 11.25 am	12.35 to 2.40 pm 12.20 to 2.55 pm	4.00 to 5.20 pm 4.20 to 5.40 pm
		Plant rhubarb, artichokes, asparagus, sea-kale, Dutch-turnips, German greens and small salading. Earth up peas, tie up lettuce and in dry weather water seed in beds.		
MAY	8, 9, 10 23, 24, 25	7.15 am to 10.40 am 7.00 am to 10.20 pm	12.30 to 3.25 pm 12.45 to 3.10 pm	4.30 to 6.00 pm 4.20 to 6.15 pm
		Sow peas, cucumber, red beet for pickling, and a full crop of kidney beans. Transplant cabbage, winter greens, cauliflower and celery. Hoe and stake peas, water newly-planted crops.		
JUNE	6, 7, 8 21, 22, 23	6.45 am to 9.40 am 6.40 am to 9.10 pm	12.55 to 3.50 pm 1.15 to 3.20 pm	4.50 to 7.00 pm 4.30 to 7.25 pm
		Top beans and peas to assist the filling of the pods. Set kidney beans and transplant cabbage, savoy, broccoli and sow turnips. Thin out onions, leeks, parsnips and early turnips.		
JULY	6, 7, 8 21, 22, 23	6.30 am to 8.45 am 6.40 am to 9.20 am	1.20 to 3.50 pm 1.00 to 3.40 pm	5.00 to 7.40 pm 5.20 to 8.15 pm
		Sow turnips, radishes, etc. Plant out broccoli, cauliflowers, savoys, leeks and winter cabbages and earth up celery. Lift full-grown winter onions.		
AUGUST	5, 6, 7 19, 20, 21	6.50 am to 9.35 am 7.00 am to 9.40 am	1.05 to 4.15 pm 1.35 to 5.05 pm	5.40 to 8.30 pm 6.30 to 9.15 pm
		Sow early cabbages and parsley for the succeeding year, also spinach, broccoli and cauliflower to stand the winter, transplant broccoli, savoys and cauliflower.		
SEPTEMBER	3, 4, 5 17, 18, 19	7.15 am to 10.10 am 7.35 am to 10.20 pm	1.40 to 5.25 pm 1.20 to 5.10 pm	6.10 to 9.00 pm 6.20 to 8.45 pm
		Plant savoys, broccoli, cauliflowers, leeks, celery. Pull onions if tips appear drying. Prick out cabbage.		
OCTOBER	3, 4, 5 17, 18, 19	8.10 am to 10.05 am 8.00 am to 11.10 am	12.10 to 4.55 pm 12.40 to 4.10 pm	6.00 to 7.40 pm 5.30 to 6.20 pm
		Plant some radishes, early cabbages, cauliflower, mint and tarragon in frames for winter use.		
NOVEMBER	1, 2, 3 15, 16, 17	8.45 am to 11.35 am 9.00 am to 11.50 am	1.15 to 3.00 pm 1.15 to 2.50 pm	4.10 to 5.15 pm 3.30 to 4.50 pm
		Dig in ground where crops are carried off and which is not intended to plant again until spring. Shallots are readily propagated by offcuts.		
DECEMBER	1, 2, 3 15, 16, 17 30, 31	9.15 am to 11.20 pm 9.05 am to 11.10 am 9.15 am to 12.10 am	1.10 to 3.45 pm 12.50 to 3.10 pm 1.25 to 3.30 pm	
		Earth up celery. Sow small salad in warm borders, covered with mats.		

Please name FOULSHAM'S ALMANACK when replying to advertisers

Michaela
Britain's leading PSYCHIC MEDIUM
will tell you what your future holds
LOVE ★ HEALTH ★ MONEY ★ CAREER
0906 200 4714
IF BUSY CALL: 09069 14 14 28
TDS, BCM 7473, WC1N 3XX Calls cost £1/min

Katrina
BRITAIN'S MOST AMAZING PSYCHIC MEDIUM
0906 203 0328
IF BUSY CALL: 09069 111 522
KTS, BCM 7473, WC1N 3XX Calls cost £1/min.

Hugo
BRITAIN'S MOST AMAZING CLAIRVOYANT
0906 • 200 • 5932
IF BUSY CALL: 09069 111 999
TDS, BCM 7473, WC1N 3XX Calls cost £1/min.

Jade
A very genuine PSYCHIC MEDIUM
will tell you what your future holds
LOVE ★ HEALTH ★ MONEY ★ CAREER
0906 • 200 • 7617
IF BUSY CALL: 09069 111 555
TDS, BCM 7473, WC1N 3XX Calls cost £1/min

---

gardening & planting by the moon 2009

higher yields in vegetables and flowers
better flavours, stronger displays, heightened colour
nick kollerstrom
RHS Lunar Gardening Correspondent

Gardeners at RHS Wisley have proved the benefits of the lunar effect – now you can use it to enjoy the best flowers and vegetables ever in 2009.

978-0-572-03459-7   £8.99
Available from good bookshops, phone 01256 302699 or from www.foulsham.com

PSYCHIC NEWS

OVER 75 YEARS' WEEKLY REPORTING ON MEDIUMS, PSYCHICS, SPIRITUALISM, HEALING AND THE PARANORMAL.

FOR A FREE SAMPLE COPY
send your name and address to:
Psychic News, Dept. OM3,
The Coach House, Stansted Hall,
Stansted, Essex CM24 8UD
or telephone: 01279 817050
fax: 01279 817051
e-mail: pn@snu.org.uk
or visit:
www.psychicnewsbookshop.co.uk
One application per household

Select your teams with Old Moore

Football Pools Forecast for 2009

This forecast, based on a combination of planetary indications and team colours, lists the teams likely to draw on the dates given, or within two days either side. No claims to infallibility are made and readers should use their own judgement, but forecasts can help them in the final selection.

3 January
Port Vale, Millwall, Rotherham, Swansea, Blackpool.

10 January
Chesterfield, Nottingham, Bournemouth, Bolton Wanderers.

17 January
Barnet, Brentford, Sheffield Wednesday, Mansfield.

24 January
Lincoln, Grimsby, Aston Villa, Chelsea.

31 January
Gillingham, Arsenal, Huddersfield, Bury.

7 February
Fulham, West Ham, Luton, Accrington Stanley.

14 February
Burnley, Nottingham Forest, Bristol City, Coventry.

21 February
Shrewsbury, Torquay, Charlton, Darlington.

28 February
Bristol City, Tottenham, Derby County, Bury.

7 March
WBA, Manchester United, Mansfield, Notts County.

14 March
Newcastle, Aston Villa, Millwall, QPR.

21 March
Plymouth, Sunderland, Charlton, Chester.

28 March
Fulham, Stoke, Blackburn Rovers, Tottenham.

4 April
Brentford, Bristol Rovers, Leeds, Grimsby.

11 April
Bolton Wanderers, Arsenal, Leicester, Derby County.

18 April
Huddersfield, Halifax, Manchester United, Liverpool.

25 April
Portsmouth, Aston Villa, Bournemouth, Yeovil.

2 May
Southend, WBA, Leicester, Bradford, Rochdale.

9 May
York, Leyton Orient, Portsmouth, Bristol City.

16 May
Lincoln City, Bournemouth, Fulham, Millwall.

23 May
Chelsea, Stoke, Swansea, Aston Villa.

30 May
Birmingham City, Brentford, Charlton, Chester.

1 August
Sunderland, Doncaster Rovers, Bury, Blackburn Rovers.

8 August
Manchester United, Chesterfield, Barnsley, West Ham.

15 August
Portsmouth, Cardiff, Arsenal, Swindon.

22 August
Mansfield, Burnley, Tottenham, Sheffield Wednesday.

29 August
Derby County, Grimsby, Northampton, Liverpool.

5 September
Gillingham, Manchester City, WBA, Brighton.

12 September
QPR, Nottingham Forest, Bolton Wanderers, Halifax.

19 September
Arsenal, Huddersfield, Doncaster Rovers, Walsall.

26 September
Rotherham, Port Vale, Manchester United, Luton.

3 October
Blackpool, Cheltenham, Stoke, Reading.

10 October
Bournemouth, Manchester City, Leeds, Coventry.

17 October
Millwall, Bolton, Wolves, Swansea.

24 October
Middlesbrough, Charlton, Barnet, Notts County.

31 October
Birmingham City, Preston NE, Barnsley, Arsenal.

7 November
Blackpool, Yeovil, West Ham, Everton.

14 November
Portsmouth, Charlton, Chelsea, Crewe.

21 November
Northampton, Sheffield Wednesday, Swansea.

28 November
Newcastle, Aston Villa, Tranmere, Barnsley.

5 December
Lincoln, Plymouth, Brentford, Manchester United.

12 December
Mansfield, Stoke, Sheffield Wednesday, Bolton.

19 December
Rotherham, WBA, Mansfield, Fulham.

26 December
Coventry, Bournemouth, Luton, Chelsea.

Please name FOULSHAM'S ALMANACK when replying to advertisers

Whatever your star-sign **Old Moore's Horoscope Daily Astral Diary** will guide you through the ups and downs of the coming year.

♈	ARIES	21 March	–	20 April
♉	TAURUS	21 April	–	21 May
♊	GEMINI	22 May	–	21 June
♋	CANCER	22 June	–	22 July
♌	LEO	23 July	–	23 August
♍	VIRGO	24 August	–	23 September
♎	LIBRA	24 September	–	22 October
♏	SCORPIO	23 October	–	22 November
♐	SAGITTARIUS	23 November	–	21 December
♑	CAPRICORN	22 December	–	20 January
♒	AQUARIUS	21 January	–	19 February
♓	PISCES	20 February	–	20 March

These horoscopes are renowned for their accuracy, forward-looking advice and emphasis on planning. With a reading for every day of the year, there is one of these books for each sign of the Zodiac. Published by Foulsham (£4.99), Old Moore will help you make the most of the opportunities open to you in 2009.

Available (Sept. 08) from all good bookshops or on-line from www.foulsham.com
Telephone: 01256 302699 for credit card purchases + p/p
(Please state which sign you require)

FREE SILVER CHARM
(normally £5.00) with all orders from this Ad
ANCIENT MAGICAL TALISMANS
Based on potent designs, up to 3,000 years old, of the Greatest Magicians. All are traditionally prepared, and hand-finished by Occulus, the Mystic with over 35 years' experience. Now YOU too can possess one or all:
No. 57 – THE FAMOUS WISHING POUCH:
"Ask and ye shall receive"
No. 16 – for LOTTERIES & GAMBLING
No. 6 – the famous pentacle for LOVE
No. 2 – for PROTECTION from EVIL
No. 1 – for WEALTH
No. 4 – for MAGIC POWERS
No. 3 – for HEALTH
£5 each post free. Immediate despatch. With free solid silver charm, carrying pouch, free catalogue.

TALISMAN OF KING SOLOMON
The famous pentacle for Good Fortune, diamond hand-engraved in finest solid silver **£15.95**.

CATALOGUE
Send four 1st class stamps for latest illustrated 50 page catalogue of superb Talismans, Ancient Egyptian Amulets, YOUR NAME in Egyptian hieroglyphics! Miraculous Medallions, Rare Seals, Power Rings, the world's largest range of occult jewellery in solid gold and silver unobtainable elsewhere.

OCCULUS (Dept M9), Ra House,
7 The Fairways, Leamington Spa, CV32 6PU

THE PSYCHIC LINK
Celebrating 19 years as Britain's Leading Live Telephone Fortune-Telling Service

Tarot   Psychic   Clairvoyance
Your Health – Your Wealth – Your Future

For Instant Access Dial

* 0906 757 0900 *

Prefer To Use Your Credit Card?
Dial: **0141 427 7003**
Single Reading Charge £25.00
All Readings 30 minutes

All Readings are provided by Professional and Experienced Readers

All services are provided by Ferda Ltd, PO 40, G51 1NR
*Calls to our 0906 numbers are charged at only 75p per minute. Calls are recorded for your protection.

Old Moore selects the winners

Racing with the Jockeys in 2009

ASTROLOGICAL POINTERS TO POSSIBLE WINNING PERIODS

The astrologically compiled dates below are presented to race-goers in the hope that they will point the way to some successful winning periods during the 2009 racing season. Specially recommended = sr.

FAVOURABLE PERIODS FOR FLAT-RACE JOCKEYS

L. DETTORI: Born 15 December 1970. Ought to be making the most of opportunities on weight-for-age races – especially so on courses in the south. His favourable periods are: 13–15, 21, 26, 28–29 March (21 sr); 2, 10, 14–16, 21–24, 27–29 April (24 sr); 3, 4, 19–23, 31 May (19 sr); 9–10, 12, 21–23 June; 6–8, 11–13, 22, 29 July (12 sr); 5, 8, 11–12, 25–26 August (11, sr); 1–3, 8–11 15–17, 29–30 September (15–17 sr); 8–11, 16–17, 26–29 October (16 sr); 1–3 November.

R. HUGHES: Born 11 January 1973 Should do well with sprinters at meetings in the north this season. His favourable periods are: 14–16, 20–22, 25 March; 8, 15–20, 27–30 April (20, 27 sr); 2–6, 16–18, 29 May (2–6, 18, sr); 4, 9, 15–19, 22–26 June; 1, 8, 18, 22–24 July (1, 8, 22 sr); 1–3, 6–9, 12, 19–25, 28, 31 August (19, 31 sr); 2, 11, 15–18, 26 September (11 sr); 2, 7, 13, 19. 20–24, 31 October (7, 20 sr); 1–2, 13–17, 29–30 November (1–2 sr).

S. SANDERS: Born 25 September 1971. Should be watched for on three- and four-year-olds, particularly in the mid-stages of the season. His favourable periods are: 13, 15, 19, 24–26 March; 1, 9–10, 19–23, 26–30 April (26 sr); 1, 13–14, 23, 29 May (13–14 sr); 10–12, 17–18, 28–29 June (17–18 sr); 1–2, 4, 7, 15–16, 29–31 July(4, 7 sr); 1–2, 14–17, 25 August (1–2, 14–17 sr); 1–3, 7–9, 16–19, 22–24 October; 3–7, 11, 15–17, 23–24, 30 November (23–24 sr).

J.P. SPENCER: Born 8 June 1980. Could well make an impact on two- or three-year-olds throughout much of the year. His favourable periods are: 11–19, 20, 25–27, 31 March; 1–2, 5–7, 14–18, 29–30 April; 1–3, 6, 10, 16–19, 30–31 May; 1, 5, 16, 24–27 June (1, 16 sr); 6, 11,18–20, 26–29 July; 1–3, 9, 12–15, 21–25 August; 3–6, 14–15, 27–29 September (3, 29 sr); 8–9, 20, 22–23, 28–31 October; 3, 7–8, 17, 20–29 November (7–8 sr).

FAVOURABLE PERIODS FOR NATIONAL HUNT JOCKEYS

R. JOHNSON: Born 27 July 1977. May be some firm successes with 'aged' horses (over six years) this season. His favourable periods are: 4, 10, 16–19, 25 January (4,10 sr); 1, 3, 5–7,15–17, 26, 28 February (15–17 sr); 7–10, 16, 19–22, 28– 30 March (11–14 sr); 1, 9, 13, 17–19, 22–24, 30 April (1, 9 sr); 2, 5–7 May; 4, 11–16, 20, 29 August; 2–5, 15–17, 27–28 September (15–17 sr); 6, 8–11, 17, 26–27, 31 October (26–27 sr); 1, 3, 5–7, 16, 19, 26–28 October (19 sr); 5, 16–17, 21–23, 30 November (21–23 sr); 4–5, 14, 21, December (14 sr).

A. P. McCOY: Born 4 May 1974. Could easily succeed on three-year-olds, particularly colts, at northern courses. His favourable periods are: 1, 4, 5–9, 12–17 January (5–9 sr) ; 6, 8–14, 18–20, 25 February; 1–4, 10–15, 23–27 March (1–4 sr); 1–3, 14–17, 24–25 April (14–17 sr); 3, 7–8, 14, 23, 25, 30 May; 1, 3–4, 6–7, 18, 26–28 August (3–4, 18 sr) 2–4, 9, 15, 18–19, 27, 30 September (18–19 sr); 1, 4–7, 15–16, 18–25, 31 October (18 –25 sr); 8–11, 16, 17, 20–21 November; 11–18, 22 December (18 sr).

R. WALSH: Born 14 May 1979. May enjoy his best successes in southern handicaps this year. His favourable periods are: 1, 6–8, 25–26, 30 January (29 sr); 2, 3, 5–10, 16–17, 22–24, 28 February; 1, 3–5, 19–20, 16–17, 22–23, 27 (22–23 sr) March; 6–12, 20, 24–25, 27–30 April (24–25 sr); 2–6, 15, 18–20, 24–26, 31 May (18–20 sr); 2–4, 15–18, 20, 23–27 August; 1–5, 13, 22–26, 30 September (22–26 sr); 4, 10, 17–18, 24, 28–31 October (17–18 24 sr); 2–3, 11–14, 20–21, 28–30 October (20–21 sr); 1–3, 9–11, 21, 25–30 November (21 sr); 2, 6–8 December.

Please name FOULSHAM'S ALMANACK when replying to advertisers

★★★ ANNASTARSIA ★★★
Our Celebrity Astrologer and Psychic

You may know AnnaStarsia, well known psychic, astrologer and dream interpreter from Living TV *Psychic Live*, BBC *Xchange* and BBC radio. She has worked for many years as an astrologer and psychic to the stars.

I am very glad to introduce her to you as an Old Moore associate. Her style and talent are as unique as her spirited personality.

Over to you AnnaStarsia

Let my team of specially selected, gifted psychics help you today! Call now for advice on your love life – money – relationships – career. For an instant live, personal reading over the phone.

Call now on 0906 119 4020

I was at a crossroads – unhappy at work and feeling my life was in need of a boost. I was toying with the idea of a holiday and your psychic picked up on this right away. She suggested I went soon as on the journey I would meet someone who would change the course of my life and in six months I would be happily living and working in another country. I did meet a wonderful man on the flight who runs a ski resort in Austria – and I am going to work for him next season! Life is on the up and I have something to look forward to. – Heather from Altrincham

Calls cost £1.50 per minute. You must be over 18 to use this service. Consultants are available 24 hours a day, 7 days a week. All calls are recorded. Helpline: 0113 384 7008.

SUPER POOLS WINNING PLAN
Win HUGE dividends for a small stake, this top selling plan gets every score draw every week! Send SAE.

CLASSIC HORSE RACING PLAN
Pick the winners from your daily paper, 16/1, 15/2, 11/4, and make big profits all year round! Send SAE.

BEAT THE FRUIT MACHINES
Win £100s every week by using this amazing system, easily learned in just a few minutes! Send SAE.

Robert Holwill (OM)
52 Purley Bury Avenue, Purley CR8 1JD

K U M A R

World famous, only leading Indian psychic who can prove to be working in London since 1968 with thousands of satisfied clients. He can help and advise you on your problems with love, marriage, job, immigration, bad luck, examination, infertility, business or any other problems of life can be solved with guarantee and confidentiality.

Ring: 0208 8020457 for an appointment at 289 High Road, Tottenham, London N15. (One minute from Seven Sisters Tube). Mobile: 07872056591. Fax: 0208 8024837 or e-mail: surinderbatra@aol.com.

Racing with the Trainers in 2009

ASTROLOGICAL POINTERS TO POSSIBLE WINNING PERIODS

The astrologically compiled dates below are presented to race-goers in the hope that they will point the way to some successful winning periods during the 2009 racing season. Specially recommended = sr.

FAVOURABLE PERIODS FOR FLAT-RACE TRAINERS

M. R. CHANNON: Born 28 November 1948. Should do best with three-year-olds in handicaps this season. His favourable periods are: 12, 18–20, 25, 27, 31 March; 2, 5, 16–19, 22, 27–29 April (16, 27 sr); 1, 5, 9–11, 17, 28–31 May (17 sr); 4–5, 9–13, 15–19, 22–26, 28 June (15–19 sr); 4–7, 10–11, 16–17, 23–28 July (16–17 sr); 1, 4–6, 16–17, 19–21, 25 August (19–21 sr); 6–9, 13, 19, 21–22, 30 September; 3, 9, 13–15, 24, 28–31 October (13 sr); 1–2 November.

M. JOHNSTON: Born 10 October 1959. Likely to do well within the latter part of the year. His favourable periods are; 16–18, 21–22, 25, 29–30 March; 3–4, 7, 18–20, 25–28 April (25–28 sr); 1–2, 11–13, 27–28, 31 May (11–13 sr) 2–6, 8, 10–15, 23–27 June (23–27 sr); 9–13, 15–17, 22–26, 31 July (9–13 sr); 1–5, 13–15, 18, 22–25, 29 August (18 sr); 2–5, 7–9, 16–19, 23–27 September (16–19 sr); 12, 16–17, 24, 27–31 October; 1, 4 November

SIR MICHAEL STOUTE: Born 22 October 1945. Should be noted at northern venues with a preponderance of two-year-olds. His favourable periods are 18, 20, 22–25, 30 March (20, 22 sr); 7–11, 16–17, 29 April (16–17 sr); 3–4, 8–9, 16–18, 29–30 May (29–30 sr); 1, 7, 15, 26–29 June (1, 7 sr); 1–3, 6–8, 10–13, 22–25 July (1–3, 6–8 sr); 1–3, 14–17, 22, 26–28 August (14–17sr); 1–3, 8–11, 23–25, 29–30 September; 1–2, 6–9, 14–19, 22–25, October (22–25 sr); 3–6 November.

FAVOURABLE PERIODS FOR NATIONAL HUNT TRAINERS

P. NICHOLLS: Born 17 April 1962. Likely to do well in the lengthier chases throughout the season. His favourable periods are: 2–23, 5–6, 19, 21–25, 31 January; 3–4, 8–9, 19–23, 28 February; 5–8, 15–16, 20–24, 28–29 March (15–16 sr); 1–3, 7–11, 13–15, 25–26, 30 April (30 sr); 8, 9, 21–25, 29–31 May; 1–2, 14–18, 30–31 August (14–18 sr); 1–3, 7–10, 16, 25–27 September (25–27 sr); 4–6, 16–19, 22, 28–31 October (16–19, 28–31 sr); 2–4, 10–14, 21, 23–26, 29–30 November (23–26 sr); 1–4, 6–9, 15–17, 23–24 December (1–4, 6–9 sr).

JONJO O'NEILL: Born 13 April 1952. Likely to win out on the longer chases throughout the season. His favourable periods are: 2–3, 11–13, 17, 22–25, 31 January (17 sr); 1–7, 9–11, 18–20, 23, 25 February (1, 9–11sr); 1–4, 8, 11–14, 22, 24–28 March (1–4, 11–14 sr); 1–3, 7–15, 17–18, 26–30 April (26–30 sr); 1–3, 7–8, 11–17, 24–26 May; 11–14, 17–18, 23–25, 31 August (17–18 sr); 2–3, 10, 14–15, 26–27, 29 September (14–15, 29 sr); 5–6, 9–10, 21–27 October (9–10 sr); 1–2, 5–6, 13–14, 22–27 November. 1–5, 10, 13–18 December (1–5, 13–18 sr).

N. TWISTON-DAVIES: Born 11 May 1957. May do particularly well with mares this season. His favourable periods are: 1–4, 10–11, 25–27, 31 January (10–11 sr); 6–10, 21–23, 25–27 February (25–27 sr); 4–5, 8–9, 19, 20–22, 28–31 March (8–9 sr); 1–3, 6–9, 12–15, 22, 25–27 April (22 sr); 1–4, 13–16, 20–22, 28–31 May; 1–2, 7, 11–15, 18, 25–27 August; 1–3, 7–8, 16–19, 25–28, 30 September (16–19 sr); 8–11, 13–18, 22, 27–31 October (13–18 sr); 2–5, 12–15, 23–26, 29–30 November (23–26 sr); 1–2, 8–10, 12–13, 21 December (8–10 sr).

Please name FOULSHAM'S ALMANACK when replying to advertisers

Greyhound Racing Numbers for 2009
TRAP-NUMBER FORECASTS FOR POTENTIAL SUCCESS

Each area of the UK has a ruling planetary number and each month of 2009 has a prominent fortunate planetary number. This forecast is based on a combination of those numbers to provide a list of the most propitious dates for betting and the trap numbers most likely to be successful.
The table shows the main areas of the UK, listed in alphabetical order. Under each monthly heading, the first column shows the best dates for betting, and the second, shaded column gives the trap numbers for the winner and the second dog.
While making no claim to infallibility, this forecast should offer those who enjoy an occasional jaunt to greyhound race meetings a way of aligning their activities with the best planetary influences and potentially increasing their success rate.

MEETING	JAN		FEB		MAR		APRIL		MAY		JUNE		JULY		AUG		SEPT		OCT		NOV		DEC	
Birmingham	3-12	43	4-11	25	4-16	56	4-12	34	4-14	26	2-11	15	2-13	14	2-9	24	3-10	53	4-16	45	3-14	64	2-13	12
	17-30	21	15-25	35	20-27	62	16-28	52	19-28	56	17-27	32	18-29	36	14-24	31	15-26	23	20-29	31	21-28	45	18-29	53
London	4-11	52	5-13	34	2-12	45	1-14	56	4-13	41	3-15	32	5-18	12	7-15	52	3-12	16	3-10	34	2-13	32	1-11	65
	14-29	36	17-26	25	18-24	16	18-29	51	15-24	13	16-22	45	23-31	51	18-26	46	19-28	54	15-28	41	17-25	71	17-26	41
Manchester	3-12	25	3-12	26	1-10	46	5-14	56	2-11	31	3-10	24	3-15	45	4-12	35	2-13	41	5-12	31	4-15	56	2-11	42
	17-29	13	16-22	52	14-27	36	19-27	12	17-26	52	16-28	63	21-29	62	18-27	14	19-28	32	19-29	34	19-27	43	17-29	34
Newcastle	3-12	24	2-10	13	4-13	56	4-14	36	2-8	51	3-11	62	5-14	21	3-12	63	2-15	35	6-15	26	4-12	52	4-15	25
	17-27	14	14-23	23	20-28	14	20-27	32	14-28	32	17-30	41	19-28	34	19-25	41	21-30	15	19-27	14	17-28	31	20-31	14
Sheffield	3-13	16	4-12	13	2-12	23	1-11	26	4-15	13	4-12	34	1-11	46	5-13	31	2-10	25	3-14	63	4-12	35	4-15	31
	19-28	54	17-26	46	15-25	12	17-27	51	20-27	42	15-23	62	15-31	12	18-27	15	16-26	42	19-29	51	17-28	12	19-28	45
South of England	2-13	34	4-15	15	1-10	24	4-14	53	3-14	35	2-13	42	6-15	15	3-11	34	4-10	62	1-14	21	4-11	61	3-14	26
	18-28	26	19-25	26	16-27	56	19-27	41	18-28	27	18-27	53	20-28	34	16-27	12	14-24	35	17-29	34	15-28	35	19-30	36
Wales	5-11	62	3-10	43	6-14	14	5-14	23	3-12	16	1-10	25	2-13	54	4-15	61	1-12	46	4-11	51	3-14	16	5-16	24
	17-28	45	19-28	52	20-30	43	17-28	31	15-25	43	14-26	34	17-28	32	19-28	42	15-27	31	15-30	26	18-28	45	20-29	36

Incense Magic Ltd

Retail and Wholesale since 1994
Medicinal herbs, tinctures, powders & capsules
Culinary herbs, whole & ground seeds & spices
Chinese cut herbs, tinctures & powders
Essential, carrier & absolute oils
www.IncenseMagic.co.uk

Naturally gifted psychics specialising in love and relationships
We choose only the best psychics to help give you direction and guidance
Immediate Consultation
freephone 0800 058 2290
9.00am - 1.00am. Credit Card £30 for 20 min
24hr. 0906 400 7472
1580 444 537 (Eire)
£1.50 p/min from a BT land line (€2.40 ROI)
BOOK ONLINE @ www.nirvanalight.com
Text Service
Text Adam or Sam and your question to
66660
Each reply costs £1.50
18+ All calls recorded

Follow your birth sign ...

Your Lucky Lotto

The prevailing planetary influences are the basis for this astro-guide to lucky Lotto numbers in 2009. Any Lotto forecast must be fallible, but to give yourself the best chance of winning, refer to the section on your birth sign.

ARIES
BORN 21 MARCH to 20 APRIL

'Let's have it now' is your motto, and though not the most materialistic of the signs, you do like the thrill of the gamble. Doing whatever feels right could be lucky for you and this is no less true with the lottery. Be ready to change your numbers on a whim, then, for this year! Or, as a further index to a win over the next twelve months, try numbers connected to your friends or a social group of some kind.

1	2
4	9

11	14	19
34	44	45

25	26	29
43	47	49

TAURUS
BORN 21 APRIL to 21 MAY

The so-called 'money sign', Taurus loves nothing more than to add to its store of financial security and once you have it you rarely lose it. This could easily be the year when your money pot gets bigger. Taureans rarely like change too; so stick to your favourite numbers (if you have them) in 2009. As an alternative strategy over the coming twelve months, single out numbers linked to your career.

1	2
7	8

10	11	19
32	35	37

25	27	28
40	41	46

LEO
BORN 23 JULY to 23 AUGUST

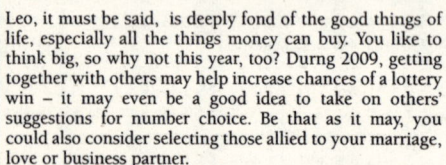

Leo, it must be said, is deeply fond of the good things of life, especially all the things money can buy. You like to think big, so why not this year, too? Durng 2009, getting together with others may help increase chances of a lottery win – it may even be a good idea to take on others' suggestions for number choice. Be that as it may, you could also consider selecting those allied to your marriage, love or business partner.

5	7
9	10

14	15	16
32	34	41

23	25	27
43	44	45

VIRGO
BORN 24 AUGUST to 23 SEPTEMBER

The Lord of Time, Saturn, still occupies your sign during 2009 and remaining faithful to the god of consistency may be the way forward. Perhaps you should chop and change numbers seldom – if at all, this year. However, as a further astrological suggestion for winning, consider numbers linked to your favourite place – work. Equally, though, anything to do with a beloved pet will suffice!

1	6
10	11

15	19	20
31	32	34

24	28	30
42	46	48

SAGITTARIUS
BORN 23 NOVEMBER to 21 DECEMBER

Sagittarius is the optimistic risk-taker par excellence, and is often quite lucky as a result. This year, the astrological picture suggests you should be aiming at some kind of stability – try to stick with favourite digits and resist the temptation for too much change. In addition, you could opt for numbers related to means of communication: your car, bus service, telephone or fax numbers.

3	6
9	12

13	15	17
30	33	38

21	22	24
39	42	48

CAPRICORN
BORN 22 DECEMBER to 20 JANUARY

With life-changing Pluto in Capricorn from the beginning of 2009, some of you are about to be transformed mightily. And why not through the Lottery? The sensible Goat, perhaps, should vary their numbers as much as possible throughout the year, unless you absolutely insist on sticking with favoured ones. However, as a further method of winning this year, choose digits related to your personal property.

1	2
5	7

8	10	11
28	37	39

13	19	20
47	48	49

... to select the winning balls

Astro-guide for 2009

Choose two numbers from the first square, then one number from each of the rectangles. Either keep to the same numbers each week, or vary the astrological indicators according to your personal vibrations.

USING THIS SYSTEM READER WINS £40,000 — MRS THERESE SINGER OF GLASGOW

GEMINI
BORN 22 MAY to 21 JUNE

This year you should be ready to embrace brand new horizons, and wouldn't a lottery win open up a few of those? Mercurial by temperament and always ready to change your mind, maybe this is the time for Gemini to hatch a plan for a regular set of numbers. However, as an extra indication to all of your numbers coming up, choose those linked to a recent holiday, favourite book or film.

2	3
8	9

12	18	19
30	31	36

21	22	29
39	45	48

CANCER
BORN 22 JUNE to 22 JULY

Cancer is one of the canniest signs when it comes to money, preferring to save rather than spend. Perhaps this naive caution is worth sticking to when it comes to how much you invest in the lottery, as is your choice of numbers. If you normally do this randomly, think about a regular set. In 2009, as a further guide to courting Lady Luck, choose numbers connected to your bank or tax details.

1	4
8	10

13	17	22
32	35	37

23	26	31
40	41	44

LIBRA
BORN 24 SEPTEMBER to 23 OCTOBER

The ruler of Libra, Venus, is often associated with minor good fortune and creature comforts. But if it's major luck you're after this year, this could well manifest if you go with intuition and change numbers around each week. And as an additional outline towards a win in 2009, you could also select numbers linked to romantic partners and your children (like anniversaries and birthdays).

5	7
8	9

14	16	19
41	43	45

22	23	32
46	47	49

SCORPIO
BORN 24 OCTOBER to 22 NOVEMBER

The revolutionary planet Uranus is now in the portion of your solar chart that 'rules' speculation and gambling. This indicates your best approach may be to remain open to change, do things spontaneously, and listen to your 'inner voice'. (Uranus is all about that archetypal flash of inspiration!) As an additional guide to winning the lottery in 2009, try numbers associated with a place of residence or your parents.

2	6
4	8

13	17	18
31	35	36

22	26	28
40	44	49

AQUARIUS
BORN 21 JANUARY to 19 FEBRUARY

Jupiter, the planet most associated with a lucky break, occupies your sign for the next year. It is time to expect the best from life, and surely that includes a lottery win! Go with any strong hunches you have, or let numbers 'appear' to you – those recurring on a certain day by chance or appearing strangely 'out of the blue'. As an alternative to all of this, select numbers pertaining *only* to yourself. (Like birthday, height, weight, age etc.).

1	2
6	8

10	11	15
25	37	38

16	20	22
39	45	48

PISCES
BORN 20 FEBRUARY to 20 MARCH

Flashes of intuition may be in the air this year for Pisces as Uranus continues its journey – a time, perhaps, to break with tradition and make unconventional choices. Why not make this apply to the Lottery, too, in 2009? Who knows what the result will be? However, as another indication to winning based on astrology, choose numbers which remind you of the past, recent or distant.

3	7
9	10

12	16	17
31	34	43

21	24	25
44	48	49

Please name FOULSHAM'S ALMANACK when replying to advertisers

Thunderball Astro-Guide for 2009

Thunderball forecasts are based on the power of the Sun and Jupiter in each zodiacal period. In a random draw there can be no guarantee, but these numbers may help to improve your chances.

First, find your Sun sign in the left-hand column. Then read across the first panel to select five numbers 1–34 for the main part of your entry. Then select one number from the second panel for the Thunderball.

ARIES 21 MARCH TO 20 APRIL	4	5	11	25	26	29	2	7	8	9
TAURUS 21 APRIL TO 21 MAY	3	7	15	21	29	33	4	10	13	14
GEMINI 22 MAY TO 21 JUNE	1	2	6	18	24	31	1	3	7	9
CANCER 22 JUNE TO 22 JULY	2	5	10	26	29	33	3	4	11	14
LEO 23 JULY TO 23 AUGUST	1	5	9	22	28	34	4	8	9	13
VIRGO 24 AUGUST TO 23 SEPTEMBER	2	8	12	20	22	27	1	2	7	14
LIBRA 24 SEPTEMBER TO 23 OCTOBER	4	6	13	21	28	31	2	3	10	12
SCORPIO 24 OCTOBER TO 22 NOVEMBER	2	3	7	22	27	30	3	6	11	12
SAGITTARIUS 23 NOVEMBER TO 21 DECEMBER	9	10	11	16	22	33	1	2	8	9
CAPRICORN 22 DECEMBER TO 20 JANUARY	1	2	7	18	20	22	4	5	8	11
AQUARIUS 21 JANUARY TO 19 FEBRUARY	5	7	12	22	21	24	2	3	9	14
PISCES 20 FEBRUARY TO 20 MARCH	2	6	12	16	18	22	1	5	6	12

Jean Genie
www.psychicjeangenie.com
Telephone, Email & Webcam Readings, Personal Horoscopes and much more.
Contact one of our fantastic Clairvoyant Mediums
pay by phone
0906 4000 430
credit card hot line
0800 9702 095
Calls cost £1.50, and are recorded, caller must be 18+. Please get bill payers permission. Text £1.50/msg.
SMS Reading Text 'cast' to **80122**

THE WITCH'S ALMANAC 2009
MARIE BRUCE

'A calendar guide to bringing magic into your life. This collection of spells, festivals and rituals helps readers influence their lives positively throughout the year'
– Daily Express

978-0-572-03458-9   £9.99
Available from good bookshops or www.foulsham.com

Please name FOULSHAM'S ALMANACK when replying to advertisers

Lucky Dates to Play Bingo in 2009
CHECK YOUR ZODIAC SIGN FOR YOUR GOOD-LUCK TIMES

ARIES (Birthdays 21 March to 20 April)
21 January to 5 June, 27 August to 8 December

TAURUS (Birthdays 21 April to 21 May)
4 January to 11 April, 6 June to 26 August, 15 October to 25 December

GEMINI (Birthdays 22 May to 21 June)
21 January to 25 March, 1 May to 3 July, 18 September to 6 December

CANCER (Birthdays 22 June to 22 July)
10 January to 19 April, 18 June to 30 September, 27 October to 27 December

LEO (Birthdays 23 July to 23 August)
1 January to 8 March, 5 May to 2 August, 17 October to 29 December

VIRGO (Birthdays 24 August to 23 September)
20 January to 17 May, 17 June to 9 October, 6 December to 18 December

LIBRA (Birthdays 24 September to 23 October)
13 January to 30 April, 28 May to 18 July, 26 August to 25 December

SCORPIO (Birthdays 24 October to 22 November)
5 January to 22 April, 14 May to 11 July, 27 August to 20 December

SAGITTARIUS (Birthdays 23 November to 21 December)
6 January to 11 April, 1 June to 31 July, 27 August to 24 December.

CAPRICORN (Birthdays 22 December to 20 January)
10 January to 16 May, 8 July to 9 October, 30 October to 26 December

AQUARIUS (Birthdays 21 January to 19 February)
13 January to 8 March, 20 April to 15 June, 31 August to 17 December

PISCES (Birthdays 20 February to 20 March)
8 January to 12 April, 20 May to 26 August, 9 September to 31 December

---

BRITISH ASTROLOGICAL & PSYCHIC SOCIETY
(Founded 1976 by Russell Grant)

Certificated Correspondence & Weekend Courses
(Full Member of A.P.A.E.)
Send 6 X 1st Class Stamps for Courses
& Registered Consultants Booklets
BAPS Dept, OMA, PO Box 5687,
MILTON KEYNES MK6 3WZ
TEL: 01908 201368
E-mail info@baps.ws & www.baps.ws

---

zodiac partners
"Let Love Be Your Destiny"

Find True Love and Happiness through our unique Spiritual Matching Service, a powerful psychic combination of Tarot Reading, Love Horoscope and Free Personal Profile in the Zodiac Partners Directory. Free Box Number contacts.

From Clairvoyant, Psychic Medium & Counsellor Caroline with Spiritual Guide & Personal Life Coach Patrick

Tel: 0844 884 9898   readings@zodiac-partners.co.uk

The Oldest Annual Publication ...

Main UK Fairs and Events 2009

Details may change after going to print, so do check with the local organiser or tourist board.

AGRICULTURAL EVENTS

Anglesey County Show: Gwalchmai 11–12 August
Bakewell Show: 5–6 August
Balmoral Show: Belfast 13–15 May
Bingley Show: Myrtle Park 9 August
Border Union Show: Springwood Park, Kelso 26–27 July
Bucks County Show: Weedon Park, nr Aylesbury 3 September
Cheshire County Show: Tabley, nr Knutsford 23–24 June
Cumberland County Show: Rickerby Park, Carlisle 18 July
Denbigh & Flint Show: The Green, Denbigh 20 August
Derbyshire County Show: Elvaston, nr Derby 28 June
Devon County Show: Westpoint, Clyst St Mary, Exeter 21–23 May
Dorset County Show: Dorchester Showground 5–6 September
Dumfries & Lockerbie Agricultural Show: Park Farm, Dumfries 1 August
East of England Autumn Show: Peterborough 11 October
East of England Show: Peterborough 19–21 June
Edenbridge & Oxted Agricultural Show: Ardenrun, Lingfield 30–31 August
Eye Show and Country Fair: 30–31 August
Great Yorkshire Show: Harrogate 14–16 July
Herts County Show: The Showground, Redbourn 23–24 May
Kent County Show: Detling, Maidstone 17–19 July
Leicester County Show: Dishley Grange Farm, Loughborough 3–4 May
Lincolnshire Show: Grange-de-Lings, Lincoln 17–18 June
Monmouthshire Show: Vauxhall Fields, Monmouth 27 August
Nantwich & South Cheshire Show: Dorfold Hall Park, Nantwich 29 July
New Forest & Hampshire Show: New Park, Brockenhurst 28–30 July
Newark & Nottingham County Show: Winthorpe, Newark 9–10 May
North Somerset Show: Wraxall, nr Bristol 4 May
Northumberland County Show: Tynedale Park, Corbridge 25 May
Oxfordshire County & Thame Show: Thame Showground 17 September
Pembrokeshire County Show: Withybush, Haverfordwest 18–20 August
Romsey Show: Broadlands 12 September
Royal Bath & West Show: Shepton Mallet 27–30 May
Royal Cornwall Show: Wadebridge 4–6 June
Royal County of Berkshire Show: Newbury Showground 19–20 September
Royal Highland Show: Ingliston, Edinburgh 25–28 June
Royal Lancashire Show: Ribchester 24–26 July (provisional)
Royal Norfolk Show: Norfolk Showground, Norwich 1–2 July
Royal Show: National Agricultural Centre, Stoneleigh Park 2–5 July (provisional)
Royal Welsh Agricultural Winter Fair: Llanelwedd, Builth Wells 30 November–1 December
Royal Welsh Show: Llanelwedd, Builth Wells 20–23 July
Shire Horse Spring Show: East of England Showground, Peterborough 14–15 March
Shropshire & West Midlands Show: Agricultural Showground, Shrewsbury 27–28 June
South of England Show: Showground, Ardingly, Haywards Heath 11–13 June
Staffordshire County Show: Stafford Showground 27–28 May
Suffolk Show: Trinity Park, Ipswich 27–28 May
Surrey County Show: Stoke Park, Guildford 25 May
Tendring Hundred Show: Lawford House Park, nr Manningtree 11 July
Three Counties Show: Malvern 12–14 June
Turriff Show: The Showground 2–3 August
United Counties Show: Nantyci Showground, Carmarthen 27 June (provisional)
Westmorland County Show: Lane Farm, Crooklands 10 September

OTHER EVENTS

Badminton Horse Trials: 7–10 May
Braemar Gathering: 5 September
Burghley Horse Trials: Burghley Park, Stamford 3–6 September

... says the *Guinness Book of World Records*

Chelsea Flower Show: 19–23 May (RHS members only first two days. Advance booking required)
Cowes Week: 1–8 August
Crufts Dog Show: NEC, Birmingham 5–8 March
Edinburgh International Festival: 14 August–6 September
Edinburgh Military Tattoo: Edinburgh Castle Esplanade 7–29 August
Golf. British Open Championship: Turnberry 16–19 July. **Amateur Championship:** Formby 15–20 June. **Senior Open:** Sunningdale 23–26 August.
Hampton Court Palace Flower Show: 7–12 July (RHS members only first two days)
Harrogate Autumn Flower Show: Great Yorkshire Showground 18–20 September
Harrogate Spring Flower Show: Great Yorkshire Showground 23–26 April
Henley Regatta: 1–5 July
Jersey Battle of Flowers: 13 August
Kent Garden Show: Kent County Showground, Detling, Maidstone 23–25 May
Llangollen International Musical Eisteddfod: 7–12 July
London Harness Horse Parade: South of England Showground, Ardingly, Haywards Heath 13 April
London International Horse Show: Olympia 15–21 December
Lord Mayor's Show: City of London 14 November
Malvern Autumn Garden & Country Show: Three Counties Showground 26–27 September
Malvern Spring Gardening Show: Three Counties Showground 7–10 May
National Amateur Gardening Show: Bath & West Showground, Shepton Mallet 4–6 September
Newark Vintage Tractor & Heritage Show: Newark Showground 14–15 November
Nottingham Goose Fair: 30 September–4 October
RHS Flower Show: Tatton Park, nr Knutsford, Cheshire 22–26 July
RHS Spring Flower Show: Cardiff 17–19 April
Royal Welsh Smallholders & Garden Festival: Llanelwedd, Builth Wells 16–17 May
Royal Windsor Horse Show: Home Park, Windsor (private grounds) 14–17 May
Shrewsbury Flower Show: Quarry Park 14–15 August
Wimbledon Lawn Tennis Championships: 22 June–5 July
Windsor Castle European Jumping and Dressage Championships: Home Park (private grounds) 25–30 August

A Message From
Paul Petulengro
The Worlds Leading Romany Astrologer & Palmist

Could YOU use a little Help & Guidance in these uncertain times ?
If the Answer is <u>YES</u> Then let me Guide you Down That Mysterious Path Ahead we call the FUTURE

Send <u>NO</u> Money: Just your Name, Address & Birth Date for your
<u>FREE</u> Romany Insight Reading.

Paul Petulengro
Casa Almendra, Las Pilas 51, LOJA, 18314
Granada, SPAIN

Or visit:
www.petulengro.com

In the 312th year of continuous publication

Lighting-up Times for 2009

Vehicle lamps must be used between sunset and sunrise. Times are in GMT, except 01.00 on 29 March to 01.00 on 25 October when they are BST (1 hour in advance). They are calculated for London (longitude 0°, latitude N.51°.5).

Day	Jan h m	Feb h m	Mar h m	Apr h m	May h m	June h m	July h m	Aug h m	Sept h m	Oct h m	Nov h m	Dec h m
1	16 32	17 20	18 10	20 03	20 53	21 38	21 51	21 18	20 16	19 07	17 03	16 25
2	16 33	17 22	18 12	20 05	20 55	21 39	21 50	21 16	20 14	19 05	17 01	16 24
3	16 35	17 23	18 14	20 07	20 57	21 40	21 50	21 14	20 11	19 03	16 59	16 24
4	16 36	17 25	18 16	20 08	20 58	21 41	21 49	21 13	20 09	19 01	16 58	16 23
5	16 37	17 27	18 17	20 10	21 00	21 42	21 49	21 11	20 07	18 58	16 56	16 23
6	16 38	17 29	18 19	20 12	21 01	21 43	21 48	21 09	20 05	18 56	16 54	16 22
7	16 39	17 31	18 21	20 13	21 03	21 44	21 48	21 07	20 02	18 54	16 53	16 22
8	16 41	17 33	18 22	20 15	21 05	21 45	21 47	21 06	20 00	18 52	16 51	16 22
9	16 42	17 34	18 24	20 17	21 06	21 45	21 46	21 04	19 58	18 49	16 49	16 22
10	16 44	17 36	18 26	20 18	21 08	21 46	21 45	21 02	19 56	18 47	16 48	16 22
11	16 45	17 38	18 28	20 20	21 09	21 47	21 45	21 00	19 53	18 45	16 46	16 21
12	16 46	17 40	18 29	20 22	21 11	21 48	21 44	20 58	19 51	18 43	16 45	16 21
13	16 48	17 42	18 31	20 23	21 13	21 48	21 43	20 56	19 49	18 41	16 44	16 21
14	16 49	17 43	18 33	20 25	21 14	21 49	21 42	20 54	19 46	18 39	16 42	16 21
15	16 51	'17 45	18 34	20 27	21 16	21 49	21 41	20 52	19 44	18 36	16 41	16 22
16	16 52	17 47	18 36	20 28	21 17	21 50	21 40	20 50	19 42	18 34	16 39	16 22
17	16 54	17 49	18 38	20 30	21 19	21 50	21 39	20 48	19 39	18 32	16 38	16 22
18	16 56	17 51	18 40	20 32	21 20	21 50	21 38	20 46	19 37	18 30	16 37	16 22
19	16 57	17 52	18 41	20 33	21 21	21 51	21 36	20 44	19 35	18 28	16 36	16 23
20	16 59	17 54	18 43	20 35	21 23	21 51	21 35	20 42	19 33	18 26	16 35	16 23
21	17 01	17 56	18 45	20 37	21 24	21 51	21 34	20 40	19 30	18 24	16 33	16 24
22	17 02	17 58	18 46	20 38	21 26	21 51	21 33	20 38	19 28	18 22	16 32	16 24
23	17 04	18 00	18 48	20 40	21 27	21 52	21 31	20 36	19 26	18 20	16 31	16 25
24	17 06	18 01	18 50	20 42	21 28	21 52	21 30	20 33	19 23	18 18	16 30	16 25
25	17 07	18 03	18 51	20 43	21 30	21 52	21 29	20 31	19 21	17 16	16 29	16 26
26	17 09	18 05	18 53	20 45	21 31	21 52	21 27	20 29	19 19	17 14	16 29	16 26
27	17 11	18 07	18 55	20 47	21 32	21 51	21 26	20 27	19 16	17 12	16 28	16 27
28	17 13	18 09	18 56	20 48	21 33	21 51	21 24	20 25	19 14	17 10	16 27	16 28
29	17 14		19 58	20 50	21 35	21 51	21 23	20 23	19 12	17 08	16 26	16 29
30	17 16		20 00	20 52	21 36	21 51	21 21	20 20	19 10	17 06	16 26	16 30
31	17 18		20 01		21 37		21 19	20 18		17 05		16 31

OLD MOORE'S ALMANACK is published in June each year and is available from WH Smith and all good newsagents and booksellers. In case of difficulty in finding a copy send a Cheque/Postal Order for £2.70 to Foulsham, The Publishing House, Bennetts Close, Slough SL1 5AP.
For advertising queries or a media pack telephone 01843 299007.

WHEELCHAIRS DIRECT
QUALITY WHEELCHAIRS FROM £160 DELIVERED
Mobility scooters, electric wheelchairs, mob walkers and accessories.
NOW! Modern stylish electric bikes from £375 delivered.
Free colour brochures.
UK phone 02890 838111 anytime.
From Republic of Ireland phone 0044 2890 838111.
Erwin, PO Box 120, Newtownabbey BT36 4HQ, UK

Free spirits Cafe
THE FREE SPIRITS CAFÉ
For friendship, penpals or romance. Books, Astrology and More!
Visit www.freespiritscafe.com
Or phone Shirley for details on 01502 587676

WEIRD AND WONDERFUL MAGICAL STUFFS: Books, Crystals, Tarot Cards, Charms, Spells and so much more – you'll wonder how you managed without us. Free catalogue RAVEN, 17 Melton Fields, Brickyard Lane, N Ferriby, E Yorks, HU14 3HE.

FUTURE FRIENDS and loving partners, all ages, UK or overseas. Magazine est 1984. No membership fees. Person to Person (OM), PO Box 40, Minehead, TA24 5YS. T: 01643 709 509.

SEEKING NEW AGE more spiritually aware introductions, circles/groups, wiccans/pagans, healing love? Soulmate? Long established occult contact Club. All areas/worldwide. Stamp to: Dion, The Golden Wheel, Liverpool L15 8HH.

REAL MAGIC for Love, Luck and Wealth plus Crystals, Oils, Spells, Talismans and much more. www.paganshop.net. Write for your FREE CATALOGUE to: Interesting Times, PO Box 58, Blackburn, BB1 9GS.

PSYCHIC PORTRAIT with reading £10. Send name/address with cheque/postal order to Lynne Mulrooney, 10 Riverside, Nantwich, Cheshire CW5 5HT.